A Primer on
Dosage Form Design

A Primer on
Dosage Form Design

Prof. N.P.S Sengar
M.Pharm, PhD

Ritesh Agrawal
M.Pharm, PGD-PPHC, DPPM

Ashwini Singh
M.Pharm

SIRT Pharmacy, Bhopal.

PharmaMed Press
An imprint of BSP Books Pvt. Ltd.
4-4-309/316, Giriraj Lane,
Sultan Bazar, Hyderabad - 500 095.

A Primer on Dosage Form Design
by N. P. S. Sengar, Ritesh Agrawal and Ashwini Singh

Eighth Reprint 2023

Published by

PharmaMed Press
An imprint of BSP Books Pvt. Ltd.
4-4-30/316, Giriraj Lane, Sultan Bazar, Hyderabad - 500 095.
Phone: 040-23445688; Fax: 91+40-23445611
E-mail: info@pharmamedpress.com
www.pharmamedpress.com/pharmamedpress.net

Printed at
Repro India Limited.

Price: Rs. 225.00
ISBN: 978-81-88449-14-9 (Paperback)

Preface

The idea is to present comprehensive treatment of science of design of dosage form, design of controlled and sustained administration of therapeutic agents with a total integration of basic concepts and application of fundamental principles of preformulation studies for designing various dosage forms.

This book is divided into seven chapters, ranging from preformulation studies and its principle factors used in design of dosage forms to the validation methods, standard operating procedures, New product Launch, process optimization, Bio-availability, *in-vivo* evaluation have been discussed in detail.

The book also provides a wide knowledge and information on stability testing and studies of its protocols in a very concised manner.

In conclusion, particular thanks are due to Mrs. Parul Sengar for her involvement in proof reading.

We are thankful to Mr. Anil shah and their staff in bringing out the first edition of this book.

Bhopal

-Authors

Contents

INTRODUCTION

WHAT IS "DOSAGE FORM DESIGN"

Drugs are rarely administered in their pure forms, and more often than not they have to be necessarily admixed with various kinds of additives resulting in their transformation into the so called 'dosage forms' or 'drug delivery systems'. Hence, in an ultimate analysis, each and every dosage form, irrespective of its final structure and nature is a combination of the drug components and an assortment of different kinds of non-drug components, collectively called as additives. The design of a dosage form is some what analogous to the design of a building, where the architect has to have a perception of the ultimate use and conveniences that the design must be necessarily provided.

OBJECTIVE

The main objective of dosage form design is to achieve a predictable therapeutic response to a drug included in a formulation which is capable of large-scale manufacture with reproducible product quality. To ensure product quality, numerous features are required:

(i) chemical and physical stability,

(ii) suitable preservation against microbial contamination if appropriate,

(iii) uniformity of dose of drug,

(iv) acceptability to users including both prescriber and patient,

(v) suitable packaging and labelling.

There are three major considerations in design of a dosage form:

1. Biopharmaceutical considerations, including factors affecting the absorption of a drug substance from different administration routes.
2. Drug factors, such as physical and chemical properties of drug substance.
3. Therapeutic considerations, including consideration of the clinical indication to be treated and patient factors.

High-quality and efficacious medicines will be formulated and prepared only when all these factors are considered and related to each other. This is the underlying principle of dosage form design.

CLASSIFICATION

The dosage forms may be classified as follows:

(i) Form-wise

(ii) Route-wise

(iii) Release rate / Target-wise

(i) *Form-wise*: Dosage forms may be classified as

(i) Solid Dosage Forms

(ii) Liquid Dosage Forms

(iii) Semi-solid Dosage Forms.

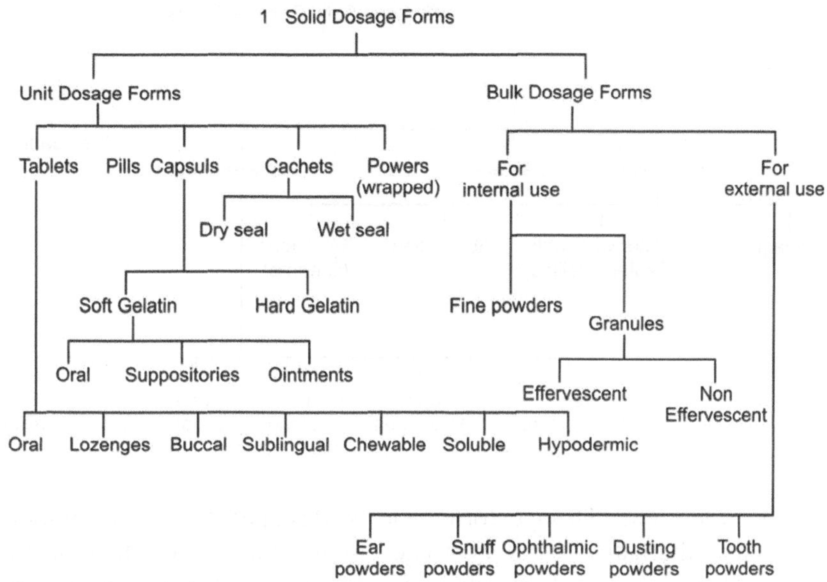
1 Solid Dosage Forms
Unit Dosage Forms
Bulk Dosage Forms
Tablets
Pills
Capsuls
Cachets
Powers (wrapped)
For internal use
For external use
Dry seal
Wet seal
Soft Gelatin
Hard Gelatin
Fine powders
Granules
Oral
Suppositories
Ointments
Effervescent
Non Effervescent
Oral
Lozenges
Buccal
Sublingual
Chewable
Soluble
Hypodermic
Ear powders
Snuff powders
Ophthalmic powders
Dusting powders
Tooth powders

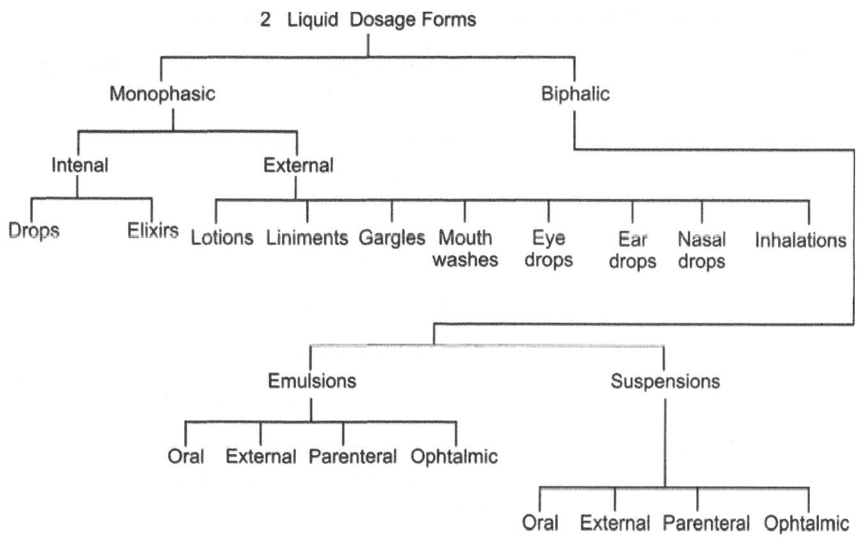
2 Liquid Dosage Forms
Monophasic
Biphalic
Intenal
External
Drops
Elixirs
Lotions
Liniments
Gargles
Mouth washes
Eye drops
Ear drops
Nasal drops
Inhalations
Emulsions
Suspensions
Oral
External
Parenteral
Ophtalmic
Oral
External
Parenteral
Ophtalmic

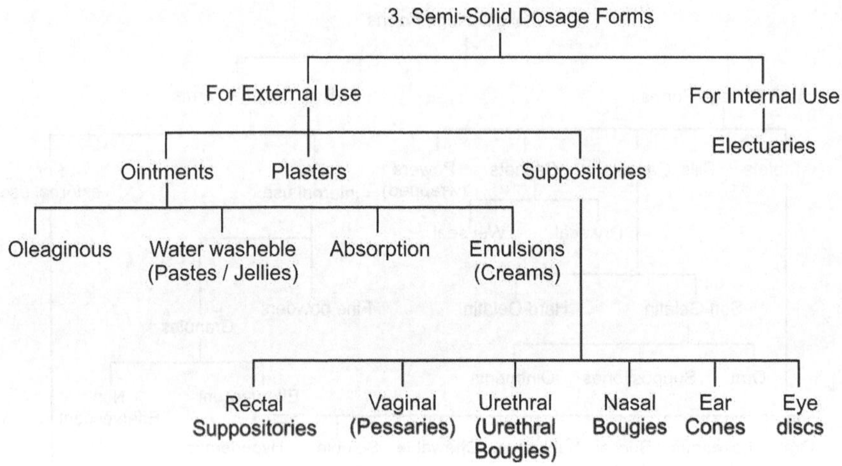

(ii) *Route-wise*: Dosage forms can be designed for administration by alternative delivery routes to maximize their therapeutic response. The following chart shows availability of dosage forms for different administration routes:

	Administration route	**Dosage Forms**
(i)	Oral	Solutions, syrups, suspensions, emulsions, gels, powders, granules, capsules and tablets.
(ii)	Rectal	Suppositories, ointments, creams, powders, solutions.
(iii)	Topical	Ointments, creams, Pastes, lotions, gels, solutions, topical aerosols.
(iv)	Nasal	Solutions, inhalations.
(v)	Eye	Solutions, ointments, creams.
(vi)	Ear	Solutions, suspensions, ointments, creams.
(vii)	Parenteral	Injections (solutions, suspension, emulsion forms), implants, irrigation and dialysis solutions.
(viii)	Respiratory	Aerosols (solution, suspension, emulsion, powder forms), inhalations, sprays, gases.

(iii) *Release Rate-wise* : Based on a release rate of a drug from its dosage form, drugs may be classified into:

(i) Sustained action

(ii) Repeat action

(iii) Prolonged action

(iv) Signal oriented

(v) Target oriented

Thus, this concludes that formulation of drugs into dosage forms requires the interpretation and application of a wide range of information from several study areas. The formulation and associated preparation of dosage forms demands the highest standard, with careful examination, analysis and evaluation of wide-ranging information by pharmaceutical scientists to achieve the objective of creating high-quality and efficacious dosage forms.

CHAPTER 1

PREFORMULATION STUDIES

PREFORMULATION

When a drug shows pharmacologic activity then preformulation studies starts. It is the first learning phase in new drug product development. In this certain physicochemical properties of the drug molecules and certain derived properties of the drug molecules are determined before preformulation studies begins physical pharmacist and medicinal chemists obtain information on the known properties of the compound and proposed development schedule as well as collect information to provide an understanding of the probable decay mechanisms and conditions that promote drug decomposition respectively.

Table 1.1 Characterization of drug in preformulation test.

	Test	Method / Function characterization
A.	Spectroscopy (UV)	Simple UV assay
B.	Solubility aqueous/ Ionizaiton constant salts; solvents partition coefficient	Phase solubility/ Purity/ pH effects, intrinsic solubility, salt formation, solubility control, hygoscopocity stability; vehicles and extraction/ lipophilicity, structure activity
C.	Melting point	Biopharmacy
D.	Assay development	DSC – Polymorphism, hydrates UV, TLC, HPLC
E.	Stability/ In solid state/ In solution	Metal ion/ thermal, hydrolysis, oxidation.
F.	Microscopy	Morphology, particle size
G.	Bulk density flow properties	Tablet and capsule formation
H.	Compression properties	Tablet and capsule formation
I.	Excipient compatibility	Excipient choice

After considering factor given in the Table 1.1 a preformulation scientist can take up the actual studies. Also analysts will generate data to confirm structure and purity given in Table 1.2.

Table 1.2 Analytical preformulation.

Attribute Test

Identity	IR, UV, TLC, DSC, NMR
Purity	Moisture, inorganic elements, heavy metals, DSC
Assay	Titration, UV, HPLC
Quality	Odour, appearance, solubility colour, melting point, pH of saturated solution

***UV spectroscopy*:** By using UV spectroscopy the acidic or basic nature of the molecule can be predicted. Choose a fixed wavelength (maximum) and quantify amount of drug present in a solution.

The absorption coefficient of the drug can be determined by formula:

$$\text{Absorbance (A)} = \log_{10}\left(\frac{I_o}{I}\right)$$

where I_o is incident light and I is transmitted light.

Above formula is based on Beers Lambert Law.

SOLUBILITY AND DISSOCIATION CONSTANT PKa

In a saturated solution at a given temperature extend to which a solute is present in dissolved state, is called its solubility. The solubility of the solute in a given solvent depends mainly on the ability of the solvent to overcome the electrical forces that bind the atoms of the solute. The solubility of substances in water can be explained on the basis of dipole nature of the water molecules. Many medicaments used today have poor solubilities and create problems during formulation. Some techniques have developed to solve this problems, micellar solubilisation, cosolvency, hydrotropy, complexation, adjustment of pH etc are the techniques which are employed to increase solubilities.

Thc solubilitics of drug in 0.1N IICl, in water and 0.1N NaOH is determined. Analytical methods that are particularly useful for solubility measurements include HPLC, UV spectroscopy, gas chromatography and fluourescence spectroscopy. For most drugs reverse phase HPLC offers an efficient and accurate means of collecting solubility data

Solubility of a substance can be determined in several ways, in one method the solvent agitated with an excess of powdered solute until there is no change in concentration. Equilibrium may be established only after sometime. In another method adding small, accurately weighed quantities of solute to a small weighed quantity of solvent until no more dissolution takes place.

By using phase–solubility Fig. 1.1 constructed between solubility Vs increasing drug: solvent ratio estimate impurity present.

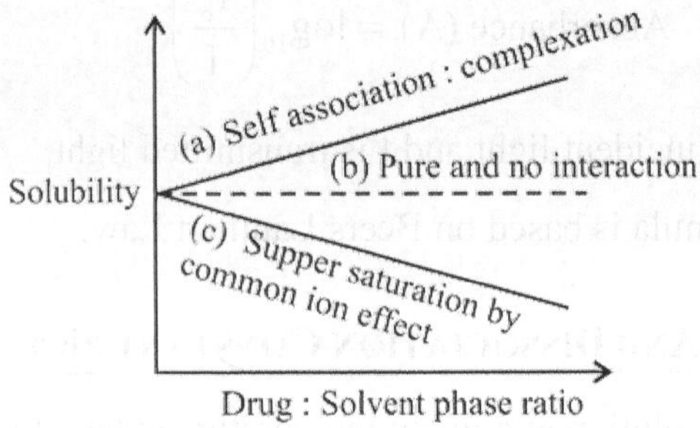

Fig. 1.1

The deviation from (saturation solubility) b indicates presence of impurities as they may increase solubility a or decrease c with increasing amount.

The solubility should be measured at 4°C and 37°C. At 4°C water is most dense, leads to a minimum aqueous solubility whereas at 37°C support biopharmaceutical evaluation.

DISSOCIATION CONSTANT pKa

Determination of pKa for a drug ionises between pH of 1–10 is important since solubility and absorption can be altered by orders of magnitude with change in pH. Most of the drugs are either weak acids or weak bases, only few drugs are non-ionic and amphoteric. The Henderson Hasselbalch equation provides an estimate of the ionized and unionized drug concentration at a particular pH.

(for acid compounds) $pH = pKa + \log\left(\frac{\text{ionized species}}{\text{unionized species}}\right)$ .....(i)

(for basic compounds) $pH = pKa + \log\left(\frac{\text{unionized species}}{\text{ionized species}}\right)$ .....(ii)

By using equation (i) and (ii)

- pKa can be determined by following changes in solubility.
- To determine solubility at any pH when intrinsic solubility and pKa are known.
- To predict the solubility and pH properties of the salts.

pKa value can be determined by a variety analytical methods. For compounds with a reasonable solubility acid–base potentiometric titrations can be performed on 100 ml portions using titrants of about 0.1 molarity.

SALTS

Solubility can be improved by forming a salt. In few cases salts prepared from strong acids or strong bases are soluble but hygroscopic, this leads to instability in tablet or capsule formation.

Various options for salt formation given in Table 1.3, to select an appropriate salt is not an easy job. The chosen salt improve solubility without causing instability and effect bioavailability of drug. A less soluble salt will less hygroscopic and form less basic or acidic solutions. Hydrochloride salts should not be used in aerosols cans as a propellant acid reaction corrode the canister. To prevent vessel or tissue damage the injections should have pH range 3–9.

SOLVENTS

Water is used as solvent. When drug insoluble in water then other solvent system used e.g., aqueous methanol used in HPLC and for extraction purpose. Oils are used in emulsion, topicals and i/m injections. Other non–aqueous solvents pharmaceutically acceptable are – ethanol and glycerol. A list of solvent given in Table 1.4.

Table 1.3 Potential pharmaceutical salts.

Basic Drugs

Anion	pKa	% usage
Hydrochloride	– 6.10	43.0
Sulphate	– 3.0, 1.96	7.5
Mesylae	– 1.20	2.0
Maleate	1.92, 6.23	3.0
Phosphate	2.15, 7.20, 12.38	3.2
Salicylate	3.0	0.9
Tartrate	3.0	3.5
Citrate	3.13, 4.76, 6.40	3.0
Succinate	4.21, 5.64	0.4
Acetate	4.76	0.4
Others	–	1.3
Lactate	3.10	0.8

Acidic Drugs

Cation	pKa	% Usage
Potassium	16.00	10.8
Sodium	14.77	6.2
Lithium	13.82	1.6
Calcium	12.90	10.5
Magnesium	11.42	1.3
Zinc	8.96	3.0
Choline	8.90	0.3
Aluminium	5.0	0.7
Others	–	8.8

Table 1.4 Recommended solvents for preformulation screening.

Solvent	Dielectric Constant(E)	Solubility(s) parameter	Application
Water	80	24.4	All
Methanol	32	14.7	Extraction separation
0.1 M HCl			Dissolution Basic extraction
0.1 M NaOH			Acidic extraction
Ethanol	24		Formulation
Propylene glycol	32	12.7	–
Glycerol	43	12.6	–
PEG 300 or 400	35	16.5	–

PARTITION COEFFICIENT

When a material is placed in an environment consisting of two or more phases it gets distributed into the phase in definite quantities depending upon its affinities for various phases. This phenomenon is known as partition and relative quantities that get distributed are expressed in the form of a ratio known as partition coefficient. The partition coefficient defined as the ratio of unionized drug distributed between the organic and aqueous phases at equilibrium

$$P_{o/w} = \frac{(C_{oil})}{(C_{water})} \text{ equilibrium}$$

Many solvents have been used as organic phase in determination of partition cocfficicnt (c.g CCl_4, IIcxanc, C_6II_6, $CIICl_3$ ctc) but n–octanol is mostly used, partition coefficient give idea of hydrophilic/ lipophilic nature of drug.

DISSOLUTION

Several physicochemical properties of a drug effects its dissolution e.g chemical form, crystal habit. Particle, size, solubility, surface area and wetting properties. The dissolution rate of a drug substance when surface area is constant during dissolution described by Noyes Whitney Equation

$$\frac{dC}{dt} = \frac{DA}{hV}(C_s - C)$$

where

D is the diffusion coefficient

A = surface area of drug exposed to dissolution media

$\frac{dC}{dt}$ = dissolution rate

V = Volume of media

h = thickness of the diffusion layer at the solid–liquid interface

C_s = Solute concentration in the diffusion layer

C = Solute concentration in bulk medium

Intrinsic dissolution rate (IDR) of a compound more than 1mg min^{-1} cm^{-2} are not likely to present dissolution rate limited absorption. Problems, IDR below 0.1mg min^{-1} cm^{-2} exhibit dissolution rate limited absorption.

POLYMORPHISM

Polymorph is defined as solid material with at least two different molecular arrangement that give distinct crystal species. Polymorph are two type first enatiotrophic (e.g sulphur) or monotropic (e.g glyceryl stearates). Polymorphs differ from each other in their various physical properties such as m.p., crystal shape, solubility, vapour pressure and electrical properties.

Polymorphism influence the bioavailability of a drug e.g., B form of chlorphenical palmitate was more bioavailable after oral administration while A and C form less bioavailable.

Polymorphs have different stability profile.

***Particle Size, Shape and Surface Area*:** Particle size change during process development. Also shape and surface area affect the stability of a drug. Griseofulvin shows higher dissolution rate and improved bioavailability on reducing the size of griseofulvin particles. Poor flow ability shown by needle shape particle. Smaller particles are prone to attack with humidity and oxygen. Then it is necessary to decide particle size range and control it during formulation.

Particle size determined by microscopy, Coulter Counter method. Measurement of surface area by Brunaver, Emmett and Teller (BET) nitrogen adsorption, in which a layer of nitrogen molecules adsorbed to the sample surface at –196°C. Surface morphology can be observed by scanning electron microscopy.

***Bulk Density*:** Bulk density of a compound varies as method of formulation vary. Knowledge of tapped density and poured density is very helpful to know size of final dosage form

$$\text{Compressibility (\%)} = \frac{\text{Tapped density} - \text{Poured density}}{\text{Tapped density}} \times 100$$

***Angle of Repose*:** A static heap of powder with only gravity acting upon it, will tend to form a conical pile. Given by this formula

$$\tan\theta = \frac{h}{r} \qquad \text{.....(a)}$$

where tan θ is angle of repose, h is height of conical pile and r is radius of conical pile.

When θ ≤ 30°, (less than 30°) free flowing and θ ≥ 40° means poor flow. Table 1.5 shows relationship between type of flow and angle of repose (degrees).

Table 1.5 Angle of repose an indication of powder flow properties.

Type of flow	Angle of repose
Excellent	< 20
Good	20–30
Passable	30–34
Very poor	> 40

Note: Addition of glidant will improve flow.

Hygroscoposity: Deliquescent substance that absorbs sufficient moisture from atmosphere to dissolve itself. Efflorescent substance that loses water to form a lower hydrate or be come unhydrous. Non–hygroscopic materials are unaffected by relative humidity

Change in moisture level of hygroscopic material can influence many parameters such as flowability, compactibility and chemical stability.

Analytical methods for monitoring the moisture level are as gravimetry, TGA, Kar Fischer titration or gas chromatography. By finding the rate and extent of moisture uptake by the drug several factors are decided, storage conditions, humidity control during manufacturing operations and nature of granulating solvents etc.

MICROSCOPY

Microscope has two major applications in pharmaceutical preformulations.

Particle size analysis

To determine crystal morphology (structure and habit), polymorphism and solvates.

COMPRESSION PROPERTIES

The compression properties of most active constituent powder are poor and required addition of compression aids.

The compression properties (plasticity, elasticity, fragmentation and punch filming propensity) for small quantities of a new drug candidate can be established by the sequence outlined in the Table 1.6. Interpretation of results as follows.

(i) ***Plastic material:*** Ductile materials deform by changing shape i.e material exhibit crushing strengths in order B>A>C would have plastic tendencies.

(ii) ***Fragmentation:*** Materials show crushing strength which are independent of the method of manufacture outline in Table 1.6. are likely to shows fragmenting properties during compression.

(iii) ***Elastic material*:** Materials like paracetamol are elastic and there is very little permanent change caused by compression, the materials recover elastically when compression force is released. An elastic body will give as follows:

A will cap or laminate, B will maintain integrity and C will cap or laminate.

If bonding is weak the compact will self destruct and top will detach (capping) or whole cylinder cracks into horizontal layers (lamination).

(iv) ***Punch filming sticking*:** Top and bottom surface of punch examined for drug adhesion. The punch dipped in methanol and the drug level determined higher in A and B and C produce monolayer and suppress adhesion more effectively.

Table 1.6 Scheme for evaluation of drug compression properties.

Sample code	500mg drug + 1% magnesium stearate		
	A	**B**	**C**
Blend in a tumbler mix for	5 min	5 min	30 min
Compress 13 mm dia compacts in a IR hydraulic press at	75 M_{pa}	75 M_{pa}	75 M_{pa}
For dwell time of	2 s	30 s	2 s
Store tablets in a sealed container at room temperature to allow equilibrium	24 h	24 h	24 h
Perform crushing strength on tablets and record load	A N	B N	C N

Stability: The chemical aspects of formulation generally centred around the chemical stability of the drug and its compatibility with the other formulation ingredients. Packaging of the dosage form is an important contributor factor to product stability and must be an integral part of stability testing programmes for formulation stability chemical integrity. Changes involving additive and physical modification to the product must be monitored.

***Drugs classified according to their sensitive breakdown*:**

For example:

(a) Kaolin like drug stable under all conditions.

(b) Asprin like drug are stable only if handled correctly.

(c) Vitamins are moderately stable even with proper handling.

(d) Antibiotics in solution form are very unstable.

Drug substances decompose by effect of heat, light, O_2 and moisture. These affect can be minimised by using either packaging buffers, moisture resistant packaging etc.

e.g Magnesium stearate as lubricant interact with aspirin and should be avoided.

Knowledge of inherent stability of drug is important and it is utilized to decide excipients, processing parameters, storage condition and to predict shelf-life. Objective of stability study in preformulation design to identify situation, which pose threat stability to active ingredient and help to control them.

Investigation of stability at the three fronts

(a) Solid state stability (of drug alone).

(b) Solution phase stability.

(c) Compatibility studies (stability in presence of excipients).

Chemical unstability normally results from

- hydrolysis
- oxidation
- photolysis
- pyrolysis

e.g: esters, lactams, amides are prone to hydrolysis.

Physical stability is influence by physical properties of drug e.g., Amorphous materials less stable than crystalline. Denser materials are more stable to ambient stress.

Knowledge of drugs structures, properties helpful in designing the dress condition and obtaining data to predict the stability under normal storage condition.

***Bioavailability*:** When a drug is given intravenously, all the drug reaches the systemic circulation, therefore said to be 100% bio-available. However when a drug is given by the other route there is no guarantee that the whale dose will reach the systemic circulation intact. The fraction of an administered dose of the drug that reaches the systemic circulation in the unchanged form is known as the bioavailable dose. Hence the relative amount of an administered dose of a particular drug that reaches the systemic circulation intact and the rate at which this occur is known as the bio-availability.

Factors which influences bio-availability are as follows:

(i) ***Physicochemical factors:*** Particle size, wettability, hydrophilicity, crystal structure, solubilizaiton, molecular size.

(ii) ***Physiological parameters:*** Surfactants in gastric juice and bile, pH buffer capacity, bile, food components, permeability, transit, viscosity of luminal contents, motility patterns and flowrate, Gastrointestinal secretions, coadministered fluids.

CHAPTER 2

STUDY OF DIFFERENT TYPES OF FORMULATION ADDITIVES

ADDITIVES

Defined as a non-drug adjunct in a formulation with a definite function does not have therapeutic effect additives (excipients) are added to the formulation to facilitate the preparation, patient acceptability and functioning of the dosage form as a drug delivery system. Additives may be classified on the basis of function. There are various types of additives groups.

Excipients are considered to be inert, should not exert therapeutic or biological action, or modify the therapeutic effect of the drug present in the dosage form. They have ability to influence the rate and extent of absorption.

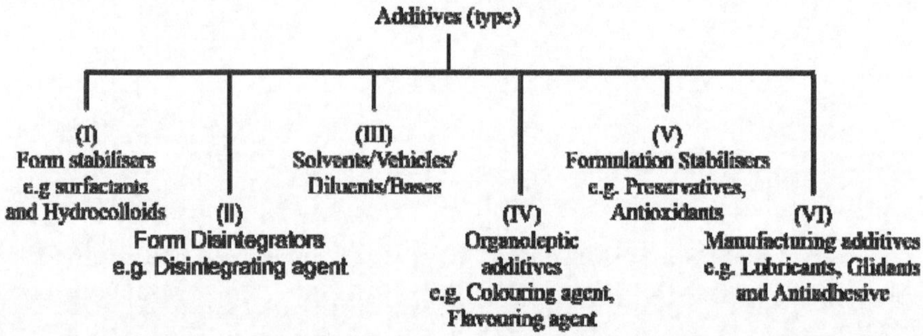

Few examples which are taken in this regard are as follows:

Diluents: Diluents may effect the bio-availability of the drug *e.g* sodium phenytoin capsules contains additives calcium sulphate dihydrate or lactose. In case of sodium phenytoin capsules with calcium sulphate as diluents bio-availability of phenytoin decreases as drug forms a poorly absorbable complex calcium–phenytoin. When some amount of phenytoin with lactose is used, an increased bio availability of phenytoin was achieved.

Lubricants: It is used in both capsules and tablets formulation to decrease the friction between the powder and metal surface during their preparation. Magnesium stearate is commonly used as a lubricant in tablets and capsules. Magnesium stearate is hydrophobic in nature in tablets reduction in dissolution rate is observed and overcomed by adding of wetting agent (water soluble surfactant) and the use of a hydrophilic diluent.

In comparison to calcium and magnesium stearate, stearic acid is a less effective lubricant than above salts and also has lower melting point.

Talc is commonly used tablet lubricants but most of its samples contain trace quantities of iron. Talc should be considered carefully in formulation of a drug whose breakdown is catalysed by the presence of iron. The higher molecular weight polyethylene glycols and certain polymeric surfactants have been used as water soluble lubricants. These materials are less effective as lubricants. Sodium stearyl fumarate is effective lubricant at low concentrations.

Glyceryl behanate: off white, tasteless powder, non-reactive with other formulation ingredients. It decreases ejection force and improves compressibility. Not sensitive to over blending, does not interfere with tablet disintegration or drug release rate, effective in the concentration range of 0.5 to 1.0%. Higher concentrations (upto 3%) may be used without any deleterious effect on the product characteristics.

***Surfactants*:** Solubilizing agents, suspension stabilizers, emulsifying agent are often used in the dosage form in the form of surfactant. Drug delivery across the biological membrane may be effected or not by the surfactant. Example surfactant monomer enhance absorption across biological membranes.

Surfactant micelles may inhibit drug absorption across biological membrane. The release of poorly soluble drug may be increased by inclusion of surfactant in the tablets or capsules formulations.

Viscosity enhancers: This agent is used in liquid preparation for ease of pouring and palatability. Complex formation between a drug and a hydrophilic polymer could decrease the drug concentration in the solution that is available for absorption.

The administration of viscous suspensions may produce an increase in viscosity of the gastro intestinal tract contents, this can decrease in the rate of movement of drug molecules to the absorbing membrane.

Diluents: Defined as inert substances used as fillers to create the desired bulk, flow properties, and compression characteristics in the preparation of tablets and capsules. Diluents (fillers) added to the formulation to produce the proper capsule fill volume e.g., cellulose, microcrystalline cellulose, starch and lactose are commonly used. In case of tablets, fillers add the necessary bulk to a formulation to prepare tablets of the desire size.

The diluents have following characteristics which are as follows:

1. Non-hygroscopic
2. Chemically inert
3. Biocompatible
4. Have an acceptable taste
5. Possess good biopharmaceutical properties e.g water soluble
6. Possess compactability and dilution capacity
7. Less costly

Lactose is the diluent mostly use in the tablet preparation. It possess the following properties.

(a) Has a pleasant taste
(b) Readily dissolve in water
(c) Non-reactive
(d) Shows good compactibility

Limitations: Some people have intolerance to lactose. Lactose exists in both crystalline and amorphous forms. Glucose, sorbitol and mannitol have been used as alternative fillers to lactose. Mannitol used in iozenges or chewable tablets, it imparts cooling sensation.

Cellulose powder also used as fillers. Cellulose are biocompatible, inert chemically, good disintegrating properties. Hygroscopic nature of cellulose may cause hydrolysis of some drugs in solid state.

Inorganic diluents such as dicalcium phosphate also used possess following properties e.g insoluble in water, non hygroscopic but hydrophilic in nature. Calcium phosphate is alkaline and incompatible to alkaline sensitive drugs. Diluents used commonly are given in the Table 2.1.

Table 2.1 Commonly used diluents.

Sugars	Inorganic compounds	Polysaccharides	Miscellaneous material
Dextrose	Calcium phosphate dihydrate	Cellulose, cellulose derivaties,	Bentonite
Lactose	Magnesium oxide	Microcystalline	Kaolin
Amylose	Calcium carbonate	cellulose, sta R $_X$ 1500, cellutab.	Silicon
Sorbitol	Magnesium carbonate	Starchess	Polyvinylpyrrolidone
Inositol	Calcium lactate trihydrate		
Sucrose	Calcium sulphate dihydrate		
Mannitol			

Binders: Tablet binders are the substances used to cause adhesion of powder particles in tablet granulations. Binder also called adhesive. Binders are added to a powder in various ways:

1. As a dry binder mixed with other excipients before compaction.
2. As a solution binder which is used as agglomeration liquid during wet agglomeration.
3. As a dry powder which is mixed with other ingredients before wet agglomeration, during agglomeration binder might thus dissolve completely or partly in the agglomeration liquid.

Binders or adhesives also maintained the integrity of the final tablet. Both dry binders and solution binders are included in the formulation typically 2–10% by weight. Example of solution binders are starch, gelatine and sucrose. Cellulose derivatives and polyvinyl pyrrolidone polymers also used as adhesive. Microcrystalline cellulose and cross linked polyvinyl pyrrolidone are used as dry binders.

Size, hardness and compressivility of granules related to nature and amount of binding agent used in granules making process. Solution binders is the most common way of incorporating a binder into granules, formed granules known as binder–substrate granules.

Natural gum, acacia and tragacanth have natural origin used as binder have variable adhesive strength and often contaminated with bacteria.

Gelatin is a nätural protein used in combination with acacia in some preparations.

Alginates and cellulose derivatives are common binders. Ethylcellulose used only as an alcoholic solution and it may retard disintegration, dissolution time of drug in the tablet when it is made by wet granulation. Table 2.2 contains commonly employed binders.

Table 2.2 Commonly used binders.

Binders	Concentration as solution %
Acacia	10–20
Bentonite	–
Carboxymethy cellulose	5–10
Gelatin	5–10
Glucose	25–50
Guar gum	10–20
Hydroxy propyl cellulose	2–10
Methyl cellulose	2–10
Polyethylene glycol	10–20
Poly saccharidic acids	5–20
Polyacrylamides	2–8
Polyvinyloxazolidones	5–10
Polyvinyl alcohols	5–20
Sorbitol	10–25
Starch paste	5–10
Tragacanth	3–10
Hydroxyl Propymethyl cellulose	2–10

Disintegrators: Disintegrators used in solid dosage forms to promote the disruption of the solid mass into smaller particles which are more readily dispersed or dissolved. When tablet placed in an aqueous solution then tablet breaks into granules, which must in turn break into fine particles.

Most disintegrators swell up in contact with water and tablet structure break into granules. Some disintegrant produce chemical changes which disintegrate the tablet such as in effervescent tablets. Cellulose and diastases constitute the other category which dissolve binding agent and cause tablet structure to break away. Release of the drug from a disintegrating tablet is shown in chart 2.1.

Most commonly used tablet disintegrants are starch, corn, potato and maize starch. Upto 10% concentration starch are included in the table formulation swelling starch in water disrupts the tablets. Disintegrants are mixed with other ingredients prior to granulation.

Clays such as veegum HV and bentonite have been used as disintegrants at about a 10% level, these materials used limited unless tablets are coloured, since clays produce an off–white appearance. Table 2.3 shown commonly used disintegrants.

Table 2.3 Commonly used tablet disintegrants.

Disintegrant	% concentration use
Alginic acid	5–10%
Clays(bentonite, Kaolin etc)	5–10%
Gum(agar, guar, karaya, pectin, tragacanth)	5–20%
Starches(pure starch like corn, potato starch, starch derivatives carboxymethyl starch, sta Rx 100)	1–10%
Cellulose(CMC,methylcellulose, MCC)	5–20%
Miscellaneous substances like resins, polymers like PVP, acid base combinations, enzymes etc	3–20%

Chart 2.1 Drug release process from a tablet by disintegration and dissolution.

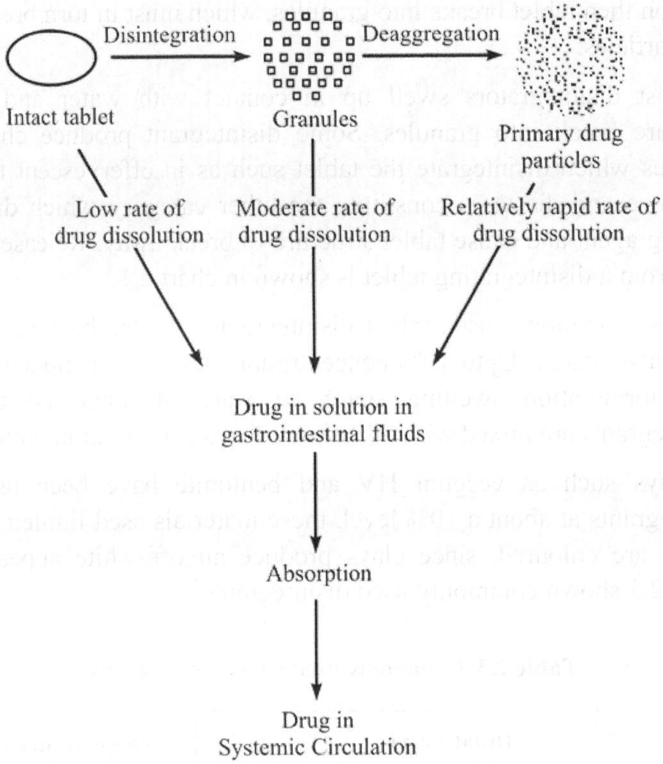

Lubricants: Defined as substances used in tablet formulations to reduce friction between powder and machine metal parts during tablet compression. Also lubricants minimize wear of the punches and dies. Lubrication is achieved by two mechanism.

MECHANISM OF LUBRICATION

1. ***Fluid lubrication***

   In this type of lubrication there is a layer of fluid between solid particles which reduces friction. Example paraffin as shown in Figs. 2.1 and 2.2.

2. ***Boundary lubrication***

In boundary lubrication a sliding surface, thin film separates the two layers and thus prevents friction. Example stearic acid salts or stearic acid

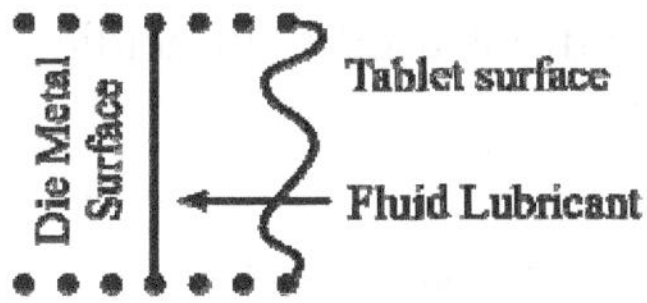

Fig. 2.1

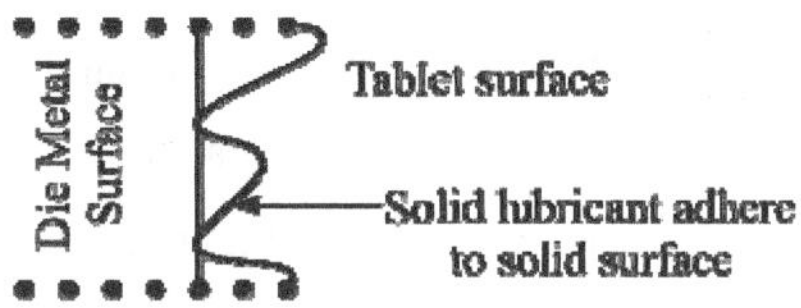

Fig. 2.2

Most lubricants are hydrophobic in nature and thus retard disintegration of the tablet, also reduces strength of the tablets. Lubricants increase the density of particle bed before compression and equalise the pressure distribution in the compressed tablets. The presence of lubricant coating on individual granules decrease the tensile strength of tablets. Lubricant with lipophilic characteristics increase dissolution time as it prevents contacts between water or fluids with granules. Hydrophobic lubricants are more effective than hydrophilic lubricants.

Lubricant selection depend upon following parameters:

(i) Type of tablet and manner in which it is to be used

(ii) Compatibility and cost

(iii) Flow properties of granules and physical properties

(iv) Anticipated dissolution qualities

Stearic acid is contra-indicated with alkaline compounds like Na_2CO_3 (sodium carbonate) due to its acidic nature. Magnesium stearate and Calcium stearate should not used with acidic drugs. Lubricants used are given in Table 2.4.

Table 2.4 Lubricants.

Material	% concentration	Material	% concentration
Boric acid	1	DL–leucine	1 – 5
Calcium stearate	1.25 – 2	Magnesium stearate	0.25 – 2
PEG 4000	1 – 5	Light liquid paraffin	1.5 – 2
PEG 6000	1 – 5	Sodium lauryl sulphate(SLS)	1 – 5
Sodium acetate	0.25 – 2	Magnesium lauryl sulphate	1 – 5
Stearic acid	0.25 – 2	Sodium chloride	5
Talcum	1 – 5		
Zinc stearate	0.25 – 2		
Vegetable oils	0.25 – 2		
Sodium benzoate	5		

SOLVENTS

Cosolvents and Vehicles

Solvent is defined as an agent to dissolve another pharmaceutic substance or a drug in the preparation of a solution. Solvents are two types – (a) Aqueous (b) Non aqueous.

Cosolvents such as water and alcohol and water and glycerin may be used when needed. Cosolvent is used to increase the solubility of poorly water soluble drug.

Vehicles defined as a carrying agent for a drug substance. They are used in formulating a variety of liquid dosage for oral and parenteral administration. Oral liquids are commonly aqueous preparation such as syrups or hydroalcoholic such as elixirs. Parenteral solution for intravenous use are aqueous, whereas intramuscular injections may be aqueous or non-aqueous.

Vehicles (for oral liquids)

1. Aqueous vehicles. Example water, purified water
2. Non-aqueous vehicles
   (a) Fixed oils of vegetable origin e.g., almond oil, arachis oil, sesame oil, soya oil and castor oil, ethyl oleate
   (b) Alcohols and polyhydric alcohols e.g., ethanol, glycerol, propylene glycol.

Cosolvents for oral liquids

Water and ethanol widely accepted. DMA has been used for parenteral product. Other solvents used are glycerol, dimethyl acetamide, ethyllactate, ethyl carbonate, 1,3-butylene glycol are reported.

Vehicles (for parenteral products)

1. Aqueous vehicles e.g., sterile water for injection, bacteriostatic water for injection, sodium chloride injection, bacteriostatic sodium chloride injection, Ringers injections, lactate ringers injections.

2. Non-aqueous vehicles
   (a) Non-aqueous water miscible vehicles e.g., ethanol, glycerine, propylene glycol etc.
   (b) Non-aqueous water immiscible vehicles e.g., fixed oils such as ethyl oleate, glycerine, propylene glycol etc.

Water: About more than 20% dosage forms listed in I.P contain water. Water is an excellent solvent. Water contains many impurities. So purified before application in pharmaceutical product manufacturing.

Non-aqueous vehicles: These are oils from plants and animals or mineral oils like various grades of liquid praffins.

Antioxidants: Defined as an agent that inhibits oxidation and thus is used to prevent the deterioration of the preparation by the oxidative process. Antioxidant which react with one or more compounds in the drug to prevent progress of the chain reaction. In general, antioxidants act by providing electrons and easily available hydrogen atoms that are accepted more readily by the free radicals than are those of drug being protected.

Antioxidants

(i) Used in aqueous preparation e.g., sodium sulphite, sodium bisulphite, phosphorous acid and ascorbic acid.

(ii) Used in oily preparation e.g., Alphatocopherol, butylhydroxylanisole, ascorbyl palmitate.

The ideal antioxidant possess the following properties:

(i) Non-volatile

(ii) Effective at low concentration

(iii) Effective over wide range of pH and stable

(iv) Odourless, colourless, non-irritant, non-sensitizing, non-toxic properties possess by antioxidants and its decomposition products

(v) Neutral – It should not react chemically with other ingredients.

Naturally occurring antioxidants are tocopherols, sesamol, guaiac resin, methionine etc.

There are a number of antioxidants which are mentioned in literature.

1. Benzoin
2. Glycerin
3. Pyrocatechol
4. Maleic acid
5. Ethyl gallate
6. Thio dipropionic acid
7. Citric acid
8. Lecithin
9. β napthol
10. Gallic acid
11. Guaic resin
12. Trihydroxy butyrophenone

Maleic acid used as rancidity retardant for oils and fats. Guaic resin good for oils and fats. Propylene glycol 70% chiefly used for foods and cosmetics.

Activity of the antioxidants can be increased by following mechanism:

(a) Complexation of trace metals that catalyse the oxidative breakdown.

(b) Lowers pH of solution thus decrease the oxidative potential.

(c) Decrease the oxygen stability of the solution.

EDTA is used as synergist material for antioxidants.

Preservatives: Defined as used in liquids and semi–solid preparations to prevent the growth of micro-organisms.

Preservative selection:

1. Should be able to prevent the growth of the wide range of microbes
2. Should be non-toxic and non-sensitising
3. Should be soluble enough in water; also in two or more phase system
4. Should be stable and non-volatile
5. Should not adversely affect the preparations container or the closure
6. Should be compatible with other ingredients of the formulation

Mode of action of preservatives: It interferes with microbial growth, multiplication and metabolism through one or more of the following mechanisms:

(a) Oxidation of cellular constituents

(b) Hydrolysis

(c) Lysis and cytoplasmic leakage

(d) Modification of cell membrane permeability and leakage of cell constituents

(e) Irreversible coagulation of cytoplasmic constituents

(f) Inhibition of cell wall synthesis

Acidic preservatives such as boric, benzoic and sorbic acids are more effective. Microbes growth below pH 3 or pH above 9, mostly in aqueous preparation so adequately preservatives are added in aqueous preparations.

These days a combination of two or more preservatives is more in fashion because such combination gives a broader spectrum of antimicrobial qualities.

Mode of action of some preservatives as follows:

1. Alcohols–lytic and denaturation action on membrane
2. Mercurials–denaturation of enzymes by combining with thiol (–SH) groups
3. Quaternary compounds–lytic action on membranes
4. Phenols–lytic and denaturation action on cytoplasmic membrane
5. Benzoic and Boric acid–denaturation of proteins

Preservation used in different pharmaceutical formulations are given in Table 2.5.

Table 2.5 Preservatives used in different pharmaceutical formulations.

Parentral Product	(% w/v)	Ophthalmic Product	(% w/v)
Benzyl alcohol	0.1–3.0	Benzalkonium chloride	0.0025–0.0133
Phenol	0.2–0.5	Thiomersal	0.001–0.5
Methyl paraben	0.1	Methyl/propyl paraben	0.05–0.01
Chlor butanol	0.25–0.5	Benzal konium chloride plus EDTA	0.01/0.1
Sodium metabisulfite	0.025–0.66		
Sodium bisulfite	0.13–0.2		
Methyl/propyl paraben	0.08–0.1/0.001–0.023		

Oral product	(% w/v)	Creams topical product	(% w/v)
Sodium benzoate	–	Benzyl alcohol	1–2
Methyl/propyl paraben	–	Methyl/propyl paraben	–
Methyl paraben	0.1	Methyl paraben	0.1–0.3
Methyl parabent + Sodium benzoate	–	Benzoic acid	0.2
		Sorbic acid	0.1
		Chlorcresol	0.05

***Suspending Agents*:** Defined as a viscosity increasing agent used to reduce the rate of sedimentation of (drug) particles dispersed throughout a vehicle in which they are not soluble. The resultant suspensions may be formulated for use orally, parenterally, opthalmically, topically or by other routes. CMC, methylcellulose, micro-crystalline cellulose, polyvinyl pyrrolidone, xanthan gum and bentonite are few of the agents employed to viscose the dispersion medium and help suspend the suspenoid.

Polymeric and hydrocolloids may render the drug in the suspension. Combinations of various types of suspending agents may be used to achieve the desired rheologic properties.

Anionic polymer sodium carboxy methyl cellulose used in parenteral preparation at concentration of 0.5%. This surfactant is incompatible with electrolytes and quiaternary ammonium compounds, it forms complexes with certain surfactants.

Synthetic polymer carbopol is used in external lotion and gel preparations.

Clays is used in the system with pH between 6–11 as suspending agent but they are stable between 9–11 pH.

With clays suspension and gel, non-ionic preservatives used e.g., paraben esters and benzoates, are useful since microbial growth in clays suspensions and gel.

***Emulsifying Agents*:** These agents are used to promote and maintain the dispersion of finely subdivided particles of a liquid in a vehicles in which it is immiscible. The end product may be a liquid emulsion or semisolid emulsion.

The choice of emulsifying agent depend upon its route of administration and its toxicity.

Emulgents are of following types

Emulsifying agents (types):

(A) ***Synthetic and Semisynthetic Emulgent:***

1. Anionic surfactants e.g., Alkali metal and ammonium soaps, sodium stearate. Soap of divalent and trivalent metals e.g., calcium oleate. Amine soaps e.g., triethonolamine stearate.
2. Cationic surfactants e.g., cetrimide.
3. Non-Ionic surfactant e.g., Glycol and Glycerol esters, Glyceryl mono stearate. Sorbital esters, lauric, oleic and stearic acid. Fatty alcohol polyglycol ethers, polyethylene glycol. Fatty acid polyglycol esters, stearate esters. Poloxalkols. Higher fatty acids, ceto stearyl alcohol.
4. Amphoteric surfactants e.g., lecithin.

(B) ***Naturally occurring materials and their derivatives:***

1. Polysaccharide e.g., Tragacanth, Sodium alginate
2. Semi-Synthetic polysaccharides

   e.g., Carnellose sodium.
3. Sterol containing substances

   e.g., wool fat, wool alcohol.

Note: Cholesterol used for w/o emulsion. Bentonite is also capable for w/o emulsion formation.

Emulsifying agents possess some or all the following properties which are as follows:

(i) Emulgent reduces surface tension upto a value of 10 dynes/cm^2.

(ii) Film formed around the disperse phase, to prevent coalescence

(iii) Should maintain zeta potential and viscosity for emulsion stability

HLB (Hydrophillic lipophillic balance) value decide the emulsifying agent type. E.g 3 to 6 HLB value lipophilic produce w/o emulsion and 8 to 18 HLB value produces o/w emulsion.

Acacia used for extemporaneous preparation. Gelatine, egg yolk for o/w emulsion. Cetyl alcohol and glyceryl monostearate for o/w emulsion. Also $Mg(OH)_2$ and $Al(OH)_3$ used for o/w emulsion preparation. HLB value of some emulgents are given in the Table 2.6.

Table 2.6 HLB value of some emulsifiers.

Agent	HLB	Agent	HLB
Surose dioleate	7.1	Sodium lauryl sulphate	40.0
Acacia	8.0	Pluronic F68	17.0
Gelatin	9.8	Tragacanth	13.2
Methyl cellulose	10.5	Triton x –15	3.6
Sodium oleate	18.0	Trito x –45	10.4
Potassium oleate	20.0	Tween 60	14.9
		Tween 80	15.0
		Tween 20	16.7

***Colouring Agent*:** These are used to impart colour to liquid and solid pharmaceutical preparations and for esthetics purpose. Most colorants in use are synthetic. Coal tar was generally used earlier. Most dyes are prepared from aniline. Both lakes and dyes have application in the colouring of sugar coated tablets, pharmaceutical suspensions, compressed (direct) tablets and other dosage forms.

Choice of colour depend upon food type and its flavour e.g., lemon flavour needs lemon colour. Rose flavour needs pink colour. Colours are uniformly mixed in the solution before application. Lake dyes give mottling on lesser occasions. The following colours are permitted according to Drug and Cosmetics Acts 1940, (DACA).

(a) Natural colour: TiO_2, annatto, carotene chlorophyll, cochineal, red and yellow oxide of iron.

(b) Artificial colours: Caramel

(c) Lakes: Al or Ca salts of any water soluble colours.

(d) Coaltar colours: Black: Napthol blue black 20470, Orange: OrangG 16230, Blue: Brilliant blue FCS 42090, Red: Sudan III 26100, Brown: Rsocrin brown 20170, Yellow: Tartrazine 19410, Green: Green S44090.

***Flavouring Agents*:** These are incorporated into a formulation to give the tablet a more pleasant taste or to mask as unpleasant one. In flavour formulating a pharmaceutical product; the pharmacist must give consideration to colour, odour, texture and taste of the preparation.

Cocoa flavoured vehicles are used for masking the taste of bitter drugs. Fruits flavours are used to combat sour or acid taste. Orange and raspberry make salty preparation palatable. Children prefer fruits flavours while adult favour tart. The match between tastes and flavours are given as:

(a) ***Alkaline taste*:** Mint, chocolate, vanilla flavour.

(b) ***Acid taste*:** Lemon, orange, liquorice, cherry flavour.

(c) ***Salty taste*:** Citrus, maple, melon flavour.

(d) ***Sweet taste*:** Fruit, honey, vanilla flavour.

(e) ***Bitter taste***: Anise, mint, fennel flavour.

(f) ***Metallic taste***: Lemon, burgundy flavour.

Sweetening Agents: These agents are used to imparts sweetness to a preparation.

Various sweetening agents are as follows:

Aspartame, glycerine, dextrose, mannitol, sorbitol, sucrose, saccharin sodium.

Sucrose is most widely used because it is colourless and soluble in water and stable over pH between 4–8. Sucrose also mask bitter taste.

Sorbitol, mannitol and glycerol included in diabetic patients. Honey and liquorice used for extemporaneous preparations.

Aspartame compound of L-aspartic acid less widely used, it has tendency to impart bitter or metallic after taste.

Saccharin and cyclamates are sweeters than sucrose solution.

Sugars promote microbial growth.

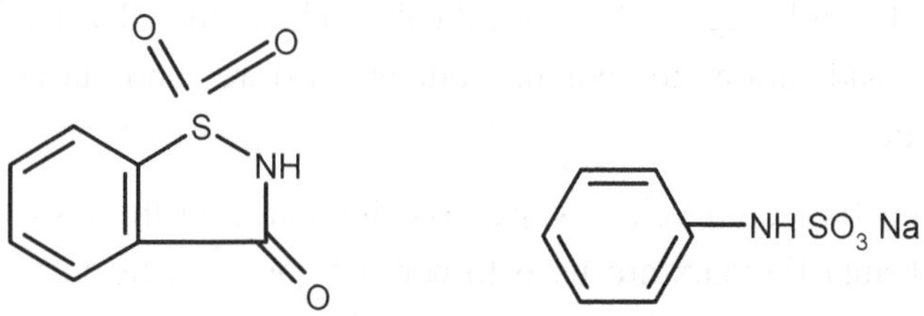

Saccharin Cyclamates

L–aspartyl phenylalanine, cyclamate, glycerrhizin, saccharin, neohesperidin dehydrochalone are sweeter than sucrose.

Viscosity Enhancers: These agents are used to change the consistency of a preparation to render it more resistant to flow. Also used in suspensions to deter sedimentation, in ophthalmic to enhance contact time, to thicken topical creams. For topical solutions viscosity enhancers are povidone, carbomer, hydroxy methyl cellulose.

Viscosity inducing polymers are known to form molecular complexes with a variety of organic or inorganic drugs and hence should be used with caution. Highly viscous solution may resist dilution by gastrointestinal tract and may affect drug release and absorption.

Examples of viscosity enhancers in various dosage forms are: Alginic acid, bentonite, carbomer, povidone, sodium alginate, tragacanth, sodium methyl cellulose, carboxymethyl cellulose.

***Materials for Ointments and Creams*:** Ointments are semisolid preparations intended for topical application to the skin or mucous membranes. Ointments are medicated and non-medicated.

ADDITIVES OF OINTMENTS

A. Ointment bases

(a) Oleaginous bases

(i) Hydro-carbons e.g., Paraffin wax.

(ii) Animal fat, vegetable oil e.g., olive oil and sesame oil.

(iii) Hydrogenated oils e.g., cotton oil (Hydrogenated).

(iv) Acid, alcohol, esters e.g., oleic acid, cetyl alcohol.

(v) Silicones e.g., dimethyl siloxanes.

(b) Absorption bases e.g., Tween 61 with vaseline

(c) Emulsion bases e.g., Beeswax + liquid paraffin + borax + water.

(d) Hydrophilic bases e.g., gelatin + glycerine + water, pectin + glycerine + normalsaline.

Descriptions of Some Ointment Bases

1. Hydrocarbon ointment bases possess the following characteristics:
   - (i) These bases are not absorbed by the skin
   - (ii) These bases prevents water loss from skin, this makes skin soft
   - (iii) They are not miscible with water, hence difficulty in removing from any body part
   - (iv) These bases retain body heat, which produces uncomfortable feeling of warmth
   - (v) These are sticky in nature, which makes cloths oily
   - (vi) They are mostly inert in nature
   - (vii) As they are stable to heat sterilization, hence suitable for sterile preparations
   - (viii) They do not support growth of microbes hence preservatives are not required
   - (ix) These bases are suitable for dry skin
   - (x) Their water absorption capacity

2. Water miscible ointment bases: Water miscible ointment bases are easily removed after water washing. As absorption bases are hydrophilic in nature but not water removable.

   Examples of water miscible bases:
   - (i) Emulsifying ointment B.P (contains anionic emulsifying wax)
   - (ii) Cetrimide emulsifying ointment B.P(contains cationic emulsifying wax)
   - (iii) Cetomacrogol emulsifying ointment B.P(contains non-ionic emulsifying wax)

These bases have following advantages which are as follows:

(i) These are used in o/w creams

(ii) Easily remove from the skin, when require

(iii) These do not interfere with physiology of skin

(iv) Miscible with wound exudates

(v) Due to presence of emulgents, these bases are in contact with skin

3. Water soluble ointment bases:

These are water soluble, prepared from macrogols(polyethylene glycols or PEGs) which are mixtures of polycondensation products of ethylene oxide and water and are described by numbers representing their average molecular weights. Their consistency vary from viscous liquids to waxy solids. Macrogols 200,300, 400 are viscous liquids, Macrogols 1500 is greasy semi solid. Macrogols 1540, 4000, 3000 are waxy solids. These are mixed in proper concentration in order to obtain proper consistency.

Advantages:

(i) Water soluble, hence water washable

(ii) Easily miscible with tissue exudates

(iii) They are non-sticky and easily spreadable

(iv) These act as solvent for many water-insoluble drugs like salicylic acid, sulphonamides and hydrocortisone

(v) They do not hydrolise, rancidify

(vi) They are compatible with many drugs such as ichthammol, zinc undecenoate, yellow mercuric oxide

(vii) These are used for drugs which are required to penetrate the skin

Disadvantages:

(i) Hygroscopic in nature, hence water sensitive drugs are not likely to be added

(ii) Benzoic, salicylic and tannic acids cause softening of the solid polymers due to complex formation. Sorbitol hardens liquid macrogols

(iii) They have limited water uptake capacity upto 5%

(iv) These reduces the activity of certain antibiotics such as penicillin, bacitracin, phenols, hydroxybenzoates

(v) Polyethylene, bakelite are dissolved in these bases hence above are not used as containers for these bases

4. Absorption bases:

These bases are hydrophilic in nature e.g., wool fat, cholesterol, beeswax etc., so have capacity to absorb certain amount of water.

Absorption bases

(i) Non-emulsified bases.

(ii) Water-in oil emulsions.

(i) Non–emulsified bases:

These bases absorb water and aqueous solutions and convert into w/o emulsions. Due to presence of sterol emulgent, they have ability to absorb water. When compared with hydrocarbon it behave differently, such as:

(a) They are less occlusive

(b) Easily spreadable

(c) These assist oil-soluble drugs to penetrate the skin

Commonly used sterol emulgents are wool fat and wool alcohols. e.g., hydrophilic petroleum U.S.P in an absorption ointment base which contains 3% cholesterol, 3% steryl alcohol, 8% beeswax and 86% white soft paraffin

(ii) Water in oil emulsions:

These bases are capable of absorbing more water and other properties are same as in case of non-emulsified absorption bases.

Examples are hydrous wool fat, (Lanolin); oily B.P cream

OTHER ADDITIVES

A. ***Preservatives***: e.g., phenylmercuric nitrate

B. ***Antioxidants***: BHA, propyl gallate, etc

C. ***Chelating agents***: citric acid, maleic acid, phosphoric acid

D. ***Perfumes***: perfume used compatible with other ingredients

Creams: Defined as semisolid preparations containing one or more medicament dissolved or dispersed in ether either an o/w emulsion or in another type water washable base. Cream consists of vehicle, base, preservatives medicament and emulsifying agent.

Classification of cream (on functional basis):

1. Cleansing and cold creams
2. Foundatoin and vanishing creams
3. Night and massage creams
4. Hand and body creams
5. All purpose and general creams.

Note:

Ointment base defined as semisolid vehicle into which drug substances may be incorporated in preparing medicated ointments.

***Suppository Bases*:** Suppositories are conveniently shaped medicated solids of various shapes and sizes suitable for insertion into one of the body orifice other than oral cavity. Suppository base used as vehicle into which drug substances are incorporated in the preparation of suppositories.

Suppository bases possess following characteristics

(i) Melt at 37°C, to disintegrate in cavities.

(ii) Non-toxic, non-irritant and non-sensitising

(iii) Should be compatible with drugs

(iv) Stable on storage

(v) Difference between solidification points and melting points be small

(vi) If base is vegetable or animal fat then its iodine value 200–245;
Acid value < 0.2; saponification value < 7.0

Types of suppository bases:

I ***Oleaginous bases***

Example: wool, fat, paraffins, olive oil, cetyl alcohol, kernel oil, soybean oil, waxes etc

II ***Water soluble bases***

(a) ***Gelato glycerin mixtures example*:** B.P 14% gelatin 70% glycerine water, U.S.P 20% gelatin and 70% glycerin + water

(b) ***Soaps glycerins example*:** Sodium stearates

(c) Polyethylene glycols–PEG 1000 96%, PEG 4000 4%, PEG 1500 70%, PEG 6000 30%

(d) Water dispersible bases, ex: tweens, span and myris etc
Tween 60 40%, Tween 61 60%, Tween 61 85%, Glyceryl laurate 15%

Suppository bases may also classified as

A. Oleaginous bases.

B. Aqueous bases. (i) Glycero gelatin bases, (ii) Macrogol bases, (iii) Soap glycerin bases.

C. Emulsifying bases

D. Synthetic fat bases.

1. ***Oleaginous bases*:**

   Cocoa butter or theobroma oil is the widely used oleaginous suppository base. It has various advantages as suppository base which are as follows:

   (i) It melts between 34–36°C, hence melts in the body.

   (ii) It is miscible with many ingredients.

   (iii) At 32°C it remains in solid state.

   (iv) On warming it becomes liquid and on cooling sets as solid.

   Disadvantages of cocoa butter:

   (i) Cocoa butter shows polymorphisms i.e.,

      (a) At temperature not above 36°C it is stable and forms 'beta' crystals

      (b) If over heated it may produce 'gamma' and alpha' crystals on cooling which melt at about 15°C and 20°C respectively

   (ii) Theobroma oil may adhere to the mould hence require lubricants

   (iii) On storage it decomposes due to oxidation of unsaturated glycerides

   (iv) It has poor water absorbing capacity, hence it is unsuitable for introducing aqueous solution of drugs

   (v) It has relatively high cost

(vi) Leakage from the body cavities such as vagina or rectum

(vii) Soluble ingredients reduced its melting point such as chloral hydrate dissolve in theobroma oil, reduce the melting point

2. ***Aqueous bases:*** These bases are water soluble and miscible

Glycerol, gelatin bases: This is mixure of glycerol, gelatin with water. This base is useful for suppositories and pessaries. Gelatin provide stiffness to the base.

Advantages:

(i) It dissolves in body secretions

(ii) It is slower, soften to mix with body secretions as compare to coca butter hence provides prolong release

Disadvantages:

(i) Difficult to handle it

(ii) It provides laxative action

(iii) It is hygroscopic in nature

(iv) As quantity of gelatin varies, there is variation in the onset of action

(v) With tannic acid, gallic acid and $FeCl_3$ gelatin is incompatible

(vi) It exists in two forms e.g., cationic and anionic

Soap–glycerin bases:

It is prepared by mixing soap and glycerin. Soap is hardening material. It possess following character which are as follows:

(i) Water soluble

(ii) Hygroscopic in nature

(iii) Not melt at body temperature

(iv) Shows therapeutic action

Macrogol Base: It is mixture of various categories of polyethylene glycols (PEGs). Possess following advantages as suppository base:

(i) Do not require cool storage as m.p above 42°C.
(ii) Suitable to handle in hot climates
(iii) Slowly release drug in the body fluids, thus used to provide prolonged action
(iv) Softness, brittleness can be reduced by using plasticizers e.g., hexane – 1, 2, 6 triol
(v) Not require lubricant
(vi) Absorbs water, hence act as solvent for drugs
(vii) Forms viscose solution on body fluid dissolution, hence leakage is not a serious problem

But it also possess some disadvantages:

(i) Highly hygroscopic in nature
(ii) Shows incompatibilities with tannins, phenols and bismuth salts
(iii) Sometimes water containing products form supersaturated solution which on storage crystallized.
(iv) Crystal growth of medicament may cause irritation
(v) Bakelite and polythene dissolve in this, hence precautions taken during container selection

3. ***Emulsifying bases:***

They are synthetic bases possess some extra qualities than other suppository bases, such as

(i) Stable not rancid
(ii) They do not adhere
(iii) Melting point not affected by over heating
(iv) Non–irritant

(v) Compatible with various medicaments

(vi) Difference between melting point and setting point is 1.5 – 2°C. Drugs not sedimented

Examples:

Witepol, massuppol, massa estarium. Above brands are popular in Britain.

4. ***Synthetic fats:***

These are developed to overcome the disadvantages of cocoa butter. Hydrogenated palm kernel oil is used as suppository base. Synthetic bases are made by first hydrolising vegetable oils, then hydrogenating the fatty acids obtained and lastly re-esterifying the acids by heating with glycerol.

These possess many advantages over theobromal oil which includes:

(i) They are unaffected by over heating

(ii) Good resistant to oxidation

(iii) Difference between melting point and setting point not more than 3°C

(iv) No lubricant is required.

(v) Due to presence of partial glycerides, its emulsifying and water absorbing capacities increases

Disadvantages:

On quickly cooling becomes brittle and less viscose than theobroma oil in melted condition hence drug sedimentation problems arises.

Many hydrocolloids such as methyl cellulose; sodium carboxy methyl cellulose can be used for water dispersible suppository bases formulation.

DRUG EXCIPIENT INTERACTIONS AND INCOMPTABILITIES

Incompatibilities defined as "Untoward result occurred by prescribing, giving or mixing of the substances and drugs which are antagonistic in nature. E.g., a number of ingredients are incompatible with polyethylene glycol bases, include benzocaine, iodochlorhydroxyquin, sulfonamides, aspirin, silver salts and tannic acid. Other materials reported to have a tendency to crystallize out of polyethylene glycol include sodium barbital, salicylic acid and camphor.

Examples of some interaction between the drug molecules and the additives are given below:

I ***Antioxidants:*** Sodium sulphide degrade thiamine by sulfite cleavage. It can convert epinephrine into sulfonic acid. It can interact with chloramphenicol by reducing its nitro group. Also addition of SO_3H to 3-ketoposition of ring A in steriod, results in loss of biological activity.

II ***Diluents, lubricants etc:*** Talcum degrade aspirin, caffeine etc., especially in presence of codeine. Calcium stearates when used as lubricants decomposes aspirin and vitamin B_{12}.

III ***Hydro-colloids:*** Alginic acid, pectin; etc., complex drug ion in liquid formulation. Carboxy methyl cellulose form complexes with neomycin and kanamycin, also with quinine.

Carrageenan forms complex with promazine, reserpine, antihistamine etc. Sodium alginate and carrageenan form insoluble salts with calcium ion.

IV ***Antimicrobial compounds:*** Quaternary ammonium compound and mercurials react with additives and cause problems.

Example: propyl paraben react with nylon used in packaging. Mercurials react with rubber stopper of solution vials. Methyl paraben, chlorbutanol react with rubber stoppers. Benzalkonium chlorides bound with tween 80, tween 20 etc.

V ***Dyes:*** Sucrose, glucose, lactose interact with blue dyes and fade its colour. Pluronic F 68, tween 20 absorb colours leading to fading.

CHAPTER 3

POLYMERS

INTRODUCTION

Polymers (biodegradable and non-biodegradable) find its application in pharmacy fields. These are widely used as pharmaceutical aids e.g., suspending agents, adhesives, coating agents etc., packaging materials and medical devices. Polymers are essential to the dispensing pharmacists, to the research pharmacists and to the manufacturing pharmacists.

DEFINITIONS

Carbon atoms can bond to one another forming the backbone of linear polymers via long chains of covalently bonded carbon atoms. Silicon and sulphur possess the same ability. Such homo-chain have the following backbone structures:

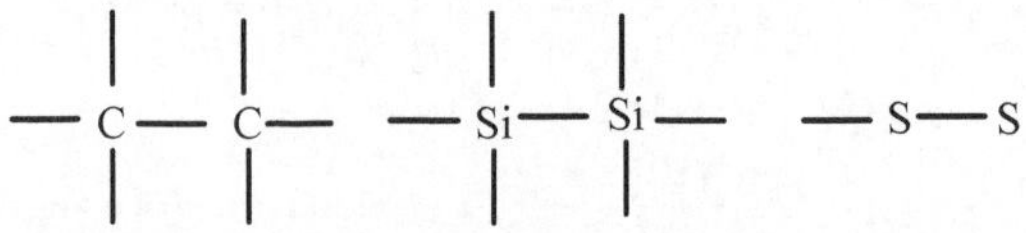

Heterochain contain other atoms in the backbone e.g.

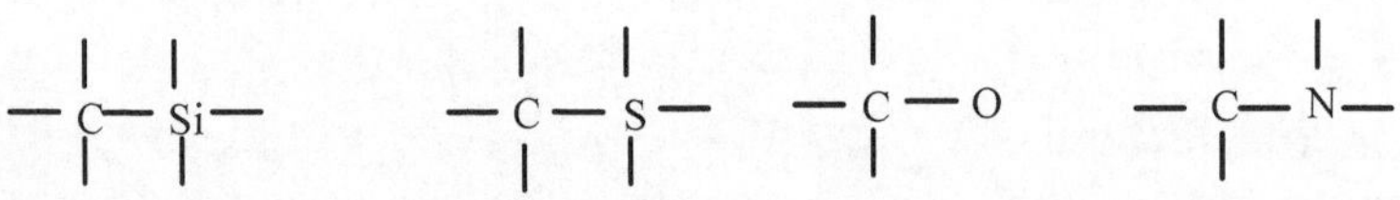

When vinyl pyrrolidone, a monomer is polymerised, it forms the linear polymer povidone USP a protective colloid capable of complexing iodine and whose aqueous solutions form strong films on drying.

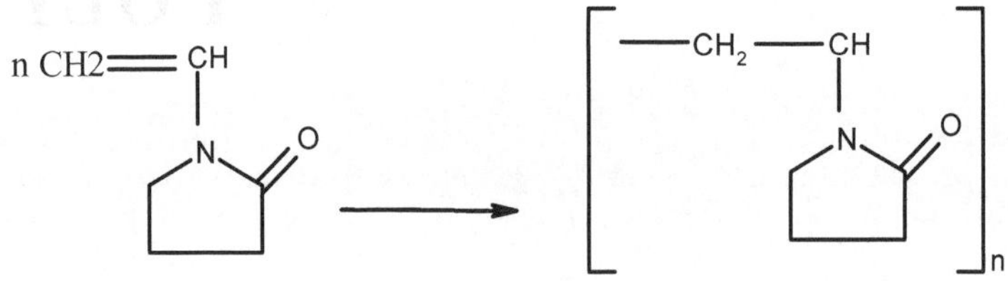

The number 'n' of repeat units per macromolecule is called the degree of polymerization. This is addition or chain reaction polymerization.

Condensation or stepwise polymerization is shown by the formation of polyethylene terephthalate, a polyster used to form fibers and films.

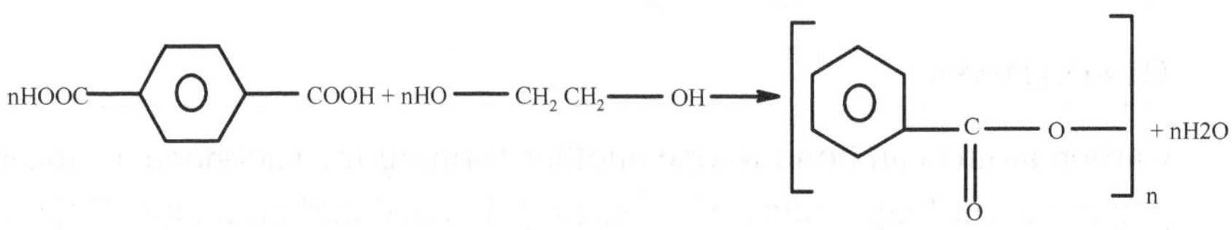

This polyesterification reaction proceeds stepwise and the molecular weight of the polymer increases gradually as the steam formed is vented from the reactor. Homopolymers consist of a single monomer, such as structure 1 to 3 copolymers incorporate two or more monomers.

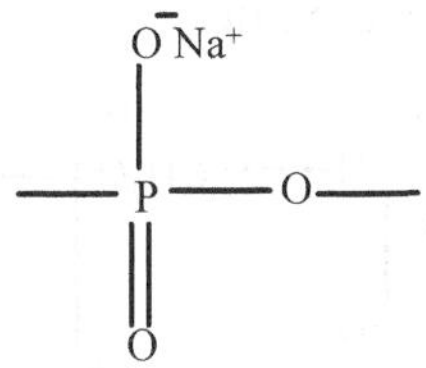

(1)

Polymeta Phosphate

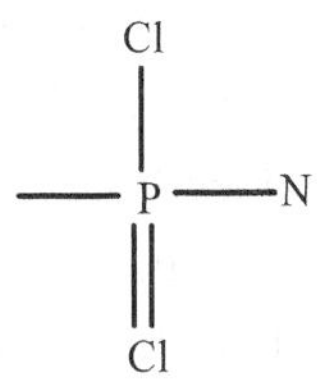

(2)

Phosphoritrile chloride

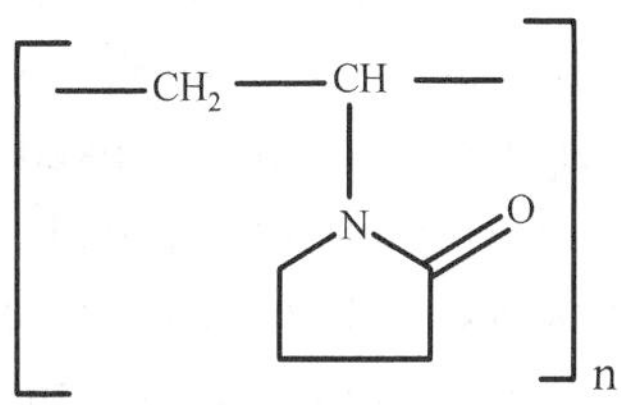

(3)

Polyvinylpyrrolidone

Cellulose and natural rubber are homopolymers but proteins are copolymers of different amino acids. Polyolefins is a random copolymer of ethylene and propylene. Polyolefins is used as a resin for containers which is used to store parenteral solutions. In alternating copolymers e.g., polypropylene sulfone made by the copolymerisation of propylene and sulphur dioxide, the two mers alternate.

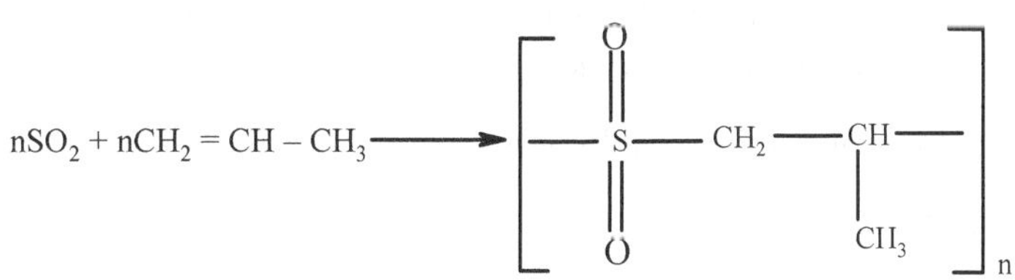

(4)

Block copolymers contain long sequences of the same mer. For instance, the fecal softener poloxakol is a block of copolymer of ethylene oxide and propylene oxide.

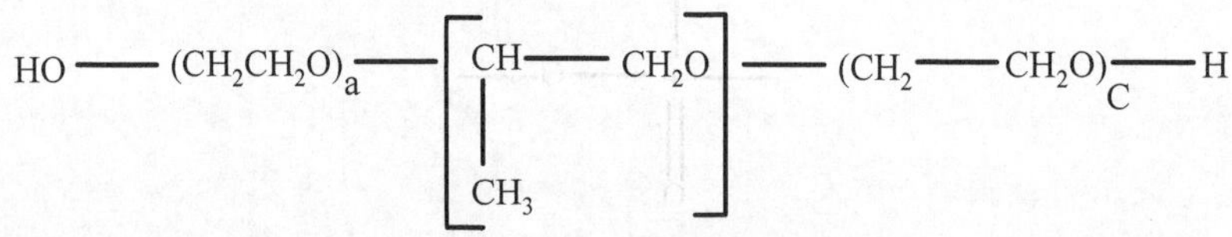

Ethylene glycol and phthalic acid are bifunctional monomers and their esterification produces the linear polymer (4). When ethylene glycol is partially or completely replaced by the trifunctional monomer glycerin, a cross linked is produced i.e., insoluble and infusible and is therefore called thermosetting. Small amount of glycerin produce a branched structure. Most linear and branched polymers are thermoplastic i.e., they can be softened or melted by heat.

CLASSIFICATION OF POLYMERS

A. Polymers based on backbone

- (i) Polymers with carbon chain backbone e.g., polyethylene, polypropylene, polystyrene, polyvinyl alcohol, polyvinyl acetate, polyacrylonitrile.
- (ii) Polymers with heterochain backbone e.g., polyethylene oxide, polypropylene oxide, cellulose, amylase, polydimethylsiloxane

B. Natural or synthetic polymers

1. Natural polymer
   - (i) Protein based e.g., Albumin, collagen, gelatine etc.
   - (ii) Polysaccharides e.g., Agarose, alginate, carrageenan, chitosan, dextran, etc.

2. Synthetic polymers

   (i) ***Biodegradable***

   Polyesters: polylactic acid, polyglycolic acid etc

   Polyanhydries: polysebacic acid, polyadipic acid, polyterphthalic acid etc.

   Polyamides: polyimino carbonates, polyamino acids etc

   Phosphorus based: polyphosphates, polyphosphonates etc

   Others: polyurethanes, polyortho esters etc

   (ii) ***Non-biodegradable*:**

   Cellulose derivatives: CMC, ethylcellulose, cellulose acetate etc.

   Silicones: colloidal silica etc

   Acrylic polymers: polymethacrylates, etc

   Others: PVP, poloxamers, poloxamines etc.

PROPERTIES OF POLYMERS

The physicochemical properties, biochemical characterization and preclinical test of a polymer must be known and carried out before application. During manufacturing process of polymer various ingredients (additives) used, methods of manufacturing and additives properties must be considered because these can degrade the drug. Surface properties such as smoothness, surface energy, hydrophilicity, lubricity affects physical properties and decide the biocompatibility with the tissue and blood. The materials for long term use must be hydrophobic to protect polymer from erosion that lead to changes in mechanical strength and toughness.

The different properties which are taken in account are as follows:

1. ***Viscosity:*** The dissolved macromolecules have ability to build up the relative viscosity of their solution e.g., USP grade methyl cellulose 2% of aqueous solution has viscosity 80 poise while water has viscosity 0.01 poise. Viscosity of polymer solutions increases exponentially with concentration. Solutions of high polymers frequently set to gels at concentration of 5% or higher. Shape of molecules decide the flow properties and solvent polymer interaction lead to significant change in solution viscosity. E.g., methyl cellulose form hydrogen bonding with water molecules, thus surrounding the polymer chain with sheath of water of hydration as chains moved, salvation layers are dragged along. The resultant increase the size of the flow units which increases the viscosity of the solution.
2. ***Solubility:*** Water soluble polymers interact with water and increase the viscosity of the solvents. Partially soluble polymers used as surgical dressing, film coating materials or as packaging materials. Higher the mol.wt. of polymer, slower its dissolution rate and greater the crystallinity of the polymer, the lower is the rate of dissolution.
3. ***Syneresis:*** Syneresis is a form of instability in aqueous gels and non-aqueous gels in this liquid separate out from a swollen gel.
4. ***Crystallinity:*** Microcrystalline cellulose is used as binder disintegrants in tablet preparation. It also form colloidal gels with water and used to form o/w emulsions (heat stable emulsion). Higher mol.wt. polymer mostly not possess crystalline structure because of difficulty in arranging chains in regular manner.

5. ***Polymer complex:*** Polymers form complexes in solution e.g., polyacids (high mol.wt.) mixed with polyglycols in water.

6. ***Interaction of polymers with solvents:*** A polymer dissolve in liquid completely or swollen by a given liquid. In cross linked polymer solution cannot occur by imbibition of liquid, polymer will swell and form gel.

7. ***Polymer dissolution:*** Dissolution of polymer in solvents is important since it has many applications e.g., drug delivery, plastics recycling, membrane science and micro lithography. Disentanglement of the polymer chains controlled polymers dissolutions.

8. ***Polymer erosion:*** Degradation of polymer is a chemical process, erosion is a physical phenomenon dependent on dissolution and diffusion process. Surface erosion occurs when the rate of erosions exceeds the rate of water permeation into the bulk of the polymer and is desirable because the kinetics of erosion and rate of drug release are highly reproducible. Bulk erosion occurs when water molecules permeate into the bulk of the matrix at a faster rate than erosion, thus exhibiting erosion kinetics.

9. ***Adsorption of macromolecules:*** Adsorption of macromolecules at the interfaces is used in suspension and emulsion stabilization. However, insulin possess this property therefore albumin is added to the insulin to prevent its absorption on the glass infusion bottles.

10. ***Bioadhesivity of water soluble polymer:*** The adhesive performance of polymers is good in case of carbopol and carboxy methyl cellulose. Adhesion between a biological surface and surface of a hydrophilic polymer arises from interactions between the polymer chains and the

macromolecules on the mucosal surface, for good adhesion there should be maximum interaction between the polymer chains of the bioadhesive and mucus.

MECHANISM OF BIODEGRADATION IN THE BODY (BIODEGRADATION OF BIODEGRADABLE POLYMERS)

Most of the polymeric implants are biodegraded by following mechanism either by hydrolysis or by oxidation during hydrolytic biodegradation there is decrease in pH while oxidative biodegradation is slow because of consumption of oxidising agents. Polyethylene carbonate biodegraded by catalytic oxidation process. During release of active agents from polymers either, diffusion, degradation and swelling process occurs. Biodegradation can be of chemical, microbial or enzymatic origin. During biodegradation these may occur separately or simultaneously, and this can also affect by following factors like absorbed and adsorbed compounds, chemical structure, configuration structure storage period, molecular weight; physical factors (shape, size etc); physicochemical factors (pH, ionic strength etc); sterilisation process, processing conditions, morphology (crystalline, amorphous), administration and site of implantation.

CHARACTERIZATION AND EVALUATION OF POLYMERS

Polymers are evaluated and characterised by following techniques.

(i) ***Glass transition***: At this temperature (Tg) amorphous changes from a solid to a liquid state. Above this temperature diffusive motion of the polymer molecules becomes possible.

(ii) ***Light scattering***: By using this method size and mobility of colloids, polymers can be determined. This is of two types – (a) static light scattering (b) dynamic light scattering.

(iii) ***Gel permeation chromatography***: In this chromatography process molecular mass and polydispersity of a polymer can be determined. Polymer sample solution pass through a column with porous packing and detectors attached with column finally measure the molecular mass.

(iv) ***Flory-Huggins parameter***: This parameter gives the energy involve in interaction of polymer with other polymers segment or with solvent molecule. Involve energy expressed in K_BT where T is temperature and K_B is boltzmann constant. Favourable interactions and unfavourable interactions given by negative value and positive value respectively.

(v) ***Isoelectric point***: Isolectric point defined as and when acidic of basic group present in a mixture of polymers then there will be a pH at which average charge is zero.

(vi) ***Differential Scanning Colorimetry***: By this instrument glass transition degree of crystallinity of semicrystalline polymer can be observed.

(vii) ***Molecular mass***: Defined as mass of polymer, mass in grams of mole of molecules and is determined by osmotic pressure, viscosity and by chemical analysis.

(viii) ***Hydrodynamic radius***: This is the radius of polymer particle in solution and determined by mobility measurement.

(ix) ***Monodisperse***: In monodisperse sample consists of molecules having identical size or mass which is synthetically difficult to achieve but occurs naturally as in DNA, proteins molecules.

(x) ***Number average molecular mass***: The number of average molecular mass is the quantity measured by determination of colligative properties such as osmotic pressure. $M_n = \frac{\Sigma n_i M_i}{\Sigma n}$

(where n_i is the number of molecules in the distribution and M_i is mass).

(xi) ***Polydispersity***: Polydispersity is the distribution of the molecular mass of the polymer and determined by M_w/M_N, where M_w is weight average molecular mass and M_n is number average molecular mass.

(xii) ***Persistence length***: This measure the stiffness of polymer. Persistence length will determine the radius of gyration of a polymer as well as the extent of entanglement that it experiences.

(xiii) ***Strain birefringence***: When a material under strain (for deformation of materials) there may be induced bire-fringence. This strain bire-fringence can be a useful tool to measure the molecular orientation in polymers.

(xiv) ***Radius of gyration***: This measures the size of a polymer molecule.

(xv) ***Tacticity***: This describes the stereochemistry of a polymer with substituent groups on each monomer. Polymer is isotactic when substituents are on the same side and syndioctactic if substituents alternate position. Atactic polymer, when there is no regular pattern of substitution. Sometimes physical properties of a polymers changed by tacticity e.g., atactic polypropylene softens at low temperature.

(xvi) ***Weight average molecular mass* (M_w)**: This is the quantity measured in an elastic light scattering experiment, which is biased towards larger molecules. M_w is always greater than M_N.

(xvii) ***Z–average molecular mass* (M_z)**: Defined as sum of $n_iM_i^3$ divided by sum of $n_im_i^2$ where n_i is the number of molecules in the distribution with mass M_i.

PHARMACEUTICAL APPLICATIONS OF POLYMERS

Polymers used as binders in tablets for viscosity and flow controlling agents in liquids, suspensions and emulsions. Polymers use as coating materials to enhance stability, mask unpleasant taste and to modify drug release properties.

Polyethylene and polyolefins bottles, styrene, vials, rubber, closures and plastic tubing for injections sets and flexible bags of plasticized polyvinyl chloride to hold blood and intravenous solutions. Barrels and plungers of hypodermic syringes are made of polypropylene. Polyester film for strip package or blister package container. Water soluble polymers such as povidone, hydroxyl propyl methyl cellulose used to coat the tablet. Some polymers such as acacia, gelatin, sodium alginate used as binders for tabletings. Ethyl cellulose with other polymers used as coating materials. A wide variety of synthetic and natural polymers are used to thicken suspension and ophthalmic solutions, as protective colloids to stabilize emulsions and suspensions and to form water soluble jellies and ointment bases.

Gelatin is a constituent of capsules, as suppository base, as emulsifying and suspending agent for absorbable films, powders and sponges, as a boot in combination with zinc oxide and for microcapsulation in combination with acacia. Sustained release (SR) dosage forms also used as polymers. Some drugs are polymers such as insulin and heparin, protamine sulphate, sodium CMC, laxatives, methyl cellulose, dextran as plasma expanders.

In addition to sutures, implants of plastics and elastomers inhuman and animal bodies are widely used for repair or replacement of tissues, organs or parts of organs.

CHAPTER 4

STABILITY STUDIES

STABILITY

Defined by USP as the extent to which a product retains within specified limits and throughout its period of storage i.e., its expiry date, the same properties and characteristics that possessed at the time of its manufacture.

In preformulation work, physical and chemical stability of a drug substance was found out since impurities present in the drug substance cause instability of drug product. Stability studies which are carried out during preformulation are as follows:

I Solution phase stability

II Solid state stability of drug alone

III Stabilityin presence of expected excipients

SOLUTION PHASE STABILITY

Solution phase stability studies are carried out to find out conditions essential for a stable solution formation during formulation. In this study following factors effects including cosolvent, light, temperature, oxygen, pH and ionic strength.

Solution stability studies at extreme pH and temperature e.g water, 0.1N NaOH at 90°C. The degraded sample assayed and given idea about rate of degradation. Cosolvents are used in parenteral preparation at appropriate pH. Once when stability solutions were prepared, then place it in flint glass ampoules. Some ampoules placed at constant temperature; some at higher temperature and light stability test are also carried out for some ampoules. Some of the sample subjected to further testing such as:

A. With an excessive head space of oxygen

B. With an inorganic antioxidant e.g $NaHSO_3$

C. With an organic antioxidant e.g BHT

D. With a head space of inert gas such as Helium

The pH based stability study using a different stimulated gastrointestinal tract condition can be designed and this idea is about stability of drug in solution phase in GI tract at different pH.

SOLID STATE STABILITY OF DRUG ALONE

Solid state stability studies used to find out, storage condition for the solid drugs and compatible excipient for the solid formulation.

Drugs (solids) are unstable because of chemical structure or their physical properties e.g., following reactions cause chemical instability like oxidation, pyrolysis, photolysis and solvolysis; unsaturated centres easily degraded by photocatalysed oxidation. Amide are easily hydrolysed as compare to esters and lactams. Amorphous materials are less stable than crystalline counter parts.

Hence knowledge of drug structures and physical properties helpful in designing the experiment for this study. Sub-parts of solid state stability are as follows:

(a) Elevated temperature studies

(b) Photolytic stability

(c) Stability to oxidation

(d) Stability under high humidity condition

STABILITY IN PRESENCE OF EXPECTED EXCIPIENTS

In this study during formulation the drug excipient interation can be obtained, which is useful for a formulator to select appropriate excipient. 5 mg of drug in a 50% excipient mixture, examine under nitrogen atmosphere at 2, 5, 10° c/min on (Digital Scanning colorimetry) over a various temperature range. Thermogram for excipients and drug used as reference appearance or disappearance of one or more peaks in thermograms of drug-excipient mixtures are considered as indication of interaction. By using TLC, interaction can be observed.

Stability testing for a drug product is carried out during its manufacturing, as a finished product. Stability studies carried out during product development are as follows:

(a) Stability testing of toxicological test samples clinical batches

(b) Drug–drug; drug excipients and drug packaging compatibility studies

(c) Stability testing of registration batches

(d) Stability testing during development and a final dosage forms including in use stability testing

Stability testing post registration:

(i) On going stability testing

(ii) Follow up stability testing

(iii) Post approval changes

(iv) Market surveillance and return stability testing

ACCELERATED STABILITY TESTING

Criteria for accepted levels of stability given in Table 4.1

Table 4.1

Sr. No.	Type of stability	Conditions maintained throughout shelf life of drug product
1	Chemical	Each active ingredient retain its chemical integrity and labelled potency within specified limits
2	Physical	The original physical properties, including appearance, palatability, uniformity, dissolution and suspendability are retained
3	Microbiological	Sterility or resistance to microbial growth is retained according to the specified requirement. Antimicrobial agents that are present retain effetiveness with in specified limits
4	Therapeutic	The therapeutic effects remains unchanged
5	Toxicological	No significant increase in toxicity occur

Pharmaceutical manufacturer has a moral legal responsibility to ensure that a formulation marketed by him reaches the consumer in an active and acceptable condition. As a formulation is liable to undergo slow deterioration on storage due to variety of internal as well as external factors, the manufacturer has to carry out preformulation and stability studies on the proposed preformulation, provide suitable overages of active ingredients, prescribe the conditions of storage and assign to it a shelf life i.e the period of which its physical, chemical, therapeutic and toxicological properties can be expected to remain within acceptable limits of quality specifications when stored under specified conditions.

Stability testing concept changes nowadays. Samples for stability testing stored under temperature with humidity conditions are selected depending upon the two factors:

I The climatic zone in which product is to be marketed

II The type of dosage forms

Geographical region of the world are defined by climatic zone which are following type:

A. Zone I temperate –(21°C/45% RH)

B. ZoneII subtropical – (25°C/60% RH)

C. Zone III hot and dry – (30°C/35% RH)

D. Zone IV hot and humid –(30°C/70% RH)

RH = Relative Humidity

Stability studies influenced by nature of drug product e.g., liquid product in semipermeable container; instable due to water loss; under dry conditions when product distributed. So tests are carried out at low humid condition under normal temperature.

For liquid product packed in impermeable containers humidity required during testing. Drugs which require refrigeration cannot tested under normal condition.

In general long term (12 months) testing conducted at 25° ± 2°C and RH 60 ± 5% samples may be retained under this condition for more than 5 years until deterioration in the sample observe. The stability testing of short term used to determine most stable product at temperature elevation in 10°C increments for 6 to 12 months. These stability studies considered with long term stability studies; then this gives drug product stability, actual shelf life and possible expiry dating.

Modern methods of stability testing make use of physicochemical principles such as reaction mechanism, order of reaction activation energies and the arrhenius equation.

These methods enable a more precise prediction of shelf life. We mostly concerned with a zero, first and pseudo first order reactions to which the arrhenius equation can be applied.

The basic plan of stability test programme is as follows:

The formulation is packed in suitable containers and they are placed in three thermostatically controlled cabinets maintained at three different temperatures e.g 37°C and 60°C. The containers are removed at suitable intervals and their contents are assayed for potency of the active ingredients. When the results i.e., the concentration of drug, are plotted against time on a graph paper, we get three lines with different slopes.

The arrhenius equation which deals with the relationship of the reaction velocity with temperature, may be stated as

$$\log K = \frac{Ha}{2.303} \times \frac{1}{T} + \log 5$$

where K → specific rate of degradation

Ha → Heat of activation

R → gas constant, 1.987 calories degrees^{-1} mol^{-1}

T → Absolute temperature

S → Collision frequency factor

When log K plotted against $\frac{1}{T}$ we can get rate constant. From the rate constant so derived the shelf life at that temperature can be calculated.

Note:

1. stability testing should be carried on the formulation packed in the container in which it is to be marketed.
2. Not all the products can be subjected to stability testing at elevated temperature e.g., exception coated tablet (protein coating), protein melt at higher temperature.
3. Full scale stability testing should be repeated when there is any change in formulation.
4. Shelf life assigned on the basis of accelerated deterioration tests should be validated later by periodical testing under field conditions of storage.

STABILITY TESTING PROTOCOLS

Accelerated stability testing requires for careful design of protocols which must define the following:

(a) Storage time before sampling

(b) The temperature and humidity for storage

(c) The number of batches to be sampled

(d) The number replicate within each batch

(e) A suitable light challenge

(f) Assay details

(g) Test parameters for evaluation of the stability samples

The objective of accelerated tests:

(a) Prediction of shelf life

(b) Detection of deterioration in product in short time

(c) Provision of a rapid means of quality

Determination of shelf life by Q_{10} method:

Shelf life can be determined by arrhenius equation as given earlier in stability testing.

The Q_{10} approach, based on E_a, is independent of reaction order and is described as:

$$Q_{10} = e^{\left\{E_a/R\left[\frac{1}{T+10}-\frac{1}{T}\right]\right\}}$$

where, E_a is energy of activation

R is the gas constant

T is the absolute temperature

Q_{10} is the ratio of two different reaction rate constant and is defined as:

$$Q_{10} = \frac{K_{(T+10)}}{K_T}$$

Q values of 2, 3 and 4 are commonly used and relate to the energies of activation of the reactions for temperature around room temperature (25°C) e.g a Q value of 2 corresponds to an E_a = 12.2 (Kcal/mol), a Q value of 3, E_a = 19.4 and a Q value of 4, E_a = 24.5

The equation to use for Q_{10} shelf life estimates is:

$$t_{90}(T_2) = \frac{t_{90}(T_1)}{Q_{10}^{(\Delta T/10)}}$$

where t_{90} (T_2) is estimated shelf life.

t_{90} (T_1) is the given shelf life at a given temperature

ΔT is the difference in temperature T_1 and T_2

As ΔT will decrease, increases the shelf life and a decrease in ΔT will increase shelf life.

OVERAGES CALCULATIONS

Overages are calculated from the accelerated stability studies and added to the preparation at the time of manufacture. Addition of overage may double the shelf life of the product. Overages added to maintain 100% of the labelled amount during the expected shelf life. 10% excess drug is added during manufacturing because 10% decomposition is permitted in the dosage form.

International Pharmaceutical Federation has recommended that overages be limited to a maximum of 30% of labelled potency of an ingredient.

Stabilization of pharmaceutical formulations:

Chemical instability e.g., alcohols, phenols, aldehydes, ketone, ester, alkaloid, glycoside etc chemically destructive process are mostly seem to two types.

General chemical destructive process (types)

(i) Hydrolysis

e.g., Aspirin, amide, lactams, lactose degrade by this process

(ii) Oxidation

e.g., aldehyde, alcohol, phenol, sugar, alkaloid fat degrade by this process.

For inorganic compound oxidation means increase in oxidation state e.g., Fe^{+2} to Fe^{+3} and for organic compound loss of H_2 from the molecules defined oxidation.

Chemical stability is important for selecting storage conditions, selecting proper container and dosage forms.

APPROACHES FOR ENHANCING STABILITY OF DRUG PRODUCTS

1. Water labile drug protected by using water proof protective coating over tablets.

(a) Water replaced by glycerine or propylene glycol.

(b) In liquid form use non-queous vehicles.

(c) Supplied drug product in dry form.

2. Use of buffering agent to protection against pH fluctuation in drug product.
3. Refrigeration of some drugs.
4. Use antioxidant e.g., $NaHSO_3$, Na_2SO_3, H_3PO_2, ascorbic acid. Note: allergic reactions produced from sulphites in asthma patients. Oxygen free environment during storage e.g., Nitrogen gas.
5. Protection from light and store in cool place e.g., In KI oral solution free radical formation from light so this is packed in opaque container as well as Na_2SO_3. 0.5gm is added in KI solution.

Polymerization, chemical decarboxylation, deamination also cause instability. E.g., formal dehyde polymerize to form $(H_2O)_n$ paraformal dehyde cause cloudy solution in container, to remove it, warm it before use.

e.g $\underset{\text{Formaldehyde}}{HCHO} \xrightarrow{(O)} \underset{\text{Formic acid}}{HCOOH}$ (tight container)

Insulin degraded in acidic environment, so neutralises the product during preparation.

Table 4.2 stability parameters for different dosage forms.

Dosage forms	Parameters
Tablets	Appearance, friability, hardness, colour, odour, moisture content and dissolution.
Capsules	Strength, moisture, colour, appearance, shape, brittleness and dissolution
Oral solutions and suspensions	Appearance, pH, colour, odour, clarity(solution), redispersibility (suspension)
Oral powders	Appearance, strength, colour, odour, moisture
Topical products (cream, lotions, solutions, gels, ointment)	Appearance, colour, odour, homogenetity, pH, strength, weight loss, resus pendibility (lotions)
Suppositories	Strength, softening range, appearance, dissolution.
Emulsions	Appearance, colour, odour, pH, viscosity, strength
Small volume parenterals (SVP)	Strength, appearance, colour, particulate matter, pH, sterility, pyrogenicity, closure integrity
Large volume parenterals (LVP)	Strength, appearance, colour, clarity, pH, volume, extractable, sterility, pyrogenicity, closure integrity
Topical non-metered aerosols	Appearance, odour, pressure, weight loss, net weight, delivery rate, spray pattern, net weight dispensed

CHAPTER 5

DESIGN, DEVELOPMENT AND PROCESS VALIDATION METHODS

LIQUID DOSAGE FORMS

In liquid oral dosage forms solvent is present in greater amount. Few exceptions are B.P syrup contains 66.7% w/w of sucrose as the solute in 33.3% of water as solvent. In most liquid dosage form solvent is in liquid form and solute may be liquid or solid.

Solvent choice: Water is mostly used as solvent but non-aqueous solvent used when drug degraded by water is used or drug that not soluble in water.

TYPES OF SOLVENT SYSTEM

Types of solvent system

- Aqueous solutions e.g. simple water, purified water, water for injections for parenteral preparations, ergotamine maleate required water free from air & Amionphylline used water free from CO_2
- Non aqueous solutions
  - (a) Fixed oils of vegetable origin e.g. Almond oil
  - (b) Alcohol e.g. C_2H_5OH, Propyl alcohol.
  - (c) Polyhydric alcohols e.g. glycerol
  - (d) Dimethyl sulphoxide used for idoxuridine (an antiviral agent)
  - (e) Ethyl ether used as a Co solvent with alcohol
  - (f) Liquid paraffin used as a solvent for topical preparation

Others non-aqueous solvents used in liquid formulations are xylene used in ear drops to dissolve ear wax, isopropylmyristate and isopropyl palmitate used as a solvent for external preparation cosmetics. Digoxin injection contain both C_2H_5OH and propylene glycol and nitrocellulose is soluble in alcohol + ether.

To improve the aqueous solubility cosolvents used, control of pH, solubilization adopted.

Other formulation additives: Buffers, density modifiers, isotonicity modifiers, viscosity enhancement, preservatives, antioxidants, sweetening agents, flavours, perfumes and colours.

Buffers: Resist change in pH of system. Borates used as external applications. Other buffering system based upon carbonates, citrates, lactates, phosphate and tartarate.

pH of body fluids (most) 7.4, buffers added in liquid preparation especially injections to avoid irritation.

Density modifiers: Most widely used material for density control is dextrose.

Isotonicity modifiers: Dextrose and NaCl used as isotonic modifiers. To avoid pain and irritation, ophthalmic preparation, parenteral preparation (LVP and SVP) made iso-osmotic with body tissue. [LVP = large volume parenteral; SVP = small volume parenteral] Others additives are described in chapter second.

Syrups: Defined as concentrated, aqueous preparations of a sugar or sugar substitute with or without flavouring agents and medicinal agent.

Types of syrup

- Non medicated syrup a (vehicles) e.g. Cherry syrup, Cocoa syrup, Orange syrup, Raspberry syrup. Non-medicated syrups (simple flavoured syrups) which do not contain any medicament but contain some pleasant flavoured substances. These syrups are used as a vehicles for other liquid preparations to mask the bitter taste of medicaments.
- Medicated syrups e.g. Meperidine HCI syrup (analgesic) Chlorpheniramine maleate syrup (Anti histamines), diphenhydramine syrup (Antitussives), Promethazine HCI syrup (Antiemetics), Guaifenesin syrup (Expectorant). Medicated syrups contain some medicinal substances along with the additives.

SYRUP COMPONENTS

1. Sugars or sugars substitute to provide viscosity and sweet taste
2. Antimicrobial preservatives
3. Flavorants
4. Colorants

Commercial syrups contains special solvents, thickness, stabilizer, solubilizing agents.

In official syrup NF which contains 85 g of sucrose in enough purified water to make syrup solution 100 ml. This preparation not required preservative because this preparation resists microbial growth. Saturated syrup solution with sucrose at cool storage shows crystalline growth and very munch unsaturated syrup shows microbial growth.

Antimicrobial preservatives: Benzoic acid (0.1 to 0.2%), sodium benzoate (0.1 to 0.2%) and combination of methyl, propyl and butyl parabens; Alcohol may be use (15–20%).

Flavorant: Flavoured with synthetic or naturally occurring materials e.g., orange oil, vanillin.

Colorant: Green with mint, brown with chocolate colours used i.e., colouring agent correlate with flavorant employed.

Preparation of Syrups

1. Solution of the ingredients with the aid of heat
2. Solution of the ingredients by agitation without aid of heat
3. Addition of sucrose to a prepared medicated liquid
4. By percolation

Formula:

Cough–Cold Syrup

Dextromethorphan hydrobromide	2.0	g
Guaifenesin	10.0	g
Chlorpheniramine maleate	0.2	g
Phenyl ephrine hydrochloride	1.0	g
Sodium benzoate	1.0	g
Saccharin sodium	1.0	g
Citric acid	1.0	g
Sodium chloride	5.2	g
Alcohol	50.0	ml
Sorbitol solution	324.0	ml
Syrup	132.0	ml
Liquid glucose	44.0	ml
Glycerine	50.0	ml
Colour	q.s.	
Flavour	q.s.	
Purified water to make	1000	ml

The oxford says, validation means, "rectification or confirmation". In process validation documented evidence that provides a high degree of assurance that a specific process will consistently produce a product that meet its predetermined specifications and quality attributes.

Chloroquin Phosphate Syrup

Each 5ml contains Chloroquin phosphate	125	mg
Equivalent of chloroquin base	78	mg
Batch size	400	litres
Practical yield	3880 × 100	ml
Usual packing	100	ml amber glass bottles

Formulation:

S.no	Ingredient	Quantity
01	Chloroquin phosphate	10 kg
02	Citric acid	4.8 kg
03	Saccharin sodium	1.6 kg
04	Glycerine	20.0 kg
05	Methyl paraben	400.0 g
06	Propyl paraben	160.0 g
07	Sugar	348.0 g
08	Essence orange	2.0 lit
09	Colour	q.s.
10	Purified water q.s	400.0 lit

1. Heat 100 lit water to 60°C–70°C in a clean stainless steel tank fitted with stirrer and bottom outlet valve. Dissolve citric acid and then dissolve sugar at 60°–70°C temperature. Heat to boiling and filter hot.

2. Heat glycerine in a stainless steel vessel to 60°C and dissolve first methyl paraben and then propyl paraben.
3. Add this solution to the main syrup.
4. Boil 44 lit water in a stainless steel vessel and to it, add 10 kg Chlorquin phosphate and stir till dissolved.
5. Add this solution to the main syrup.
6. Heat 4 lit water in a stainless steel vessel and dissolve saccharin sodium.
7. Add this to the main syrup and stir well.
8. Make–up the volume to 400 litres with water.
9. Heat 100ml water in a beaker and dissolve 4 g colour.
10. Add this to the main bulk. Stir well and allow to cool to room temperature.
11. Add essence orange.
12. Filter the syrup before filling.

Diphen Hydramine Hydro Chloride Elixir

Labelled formula:

Each 5ml contains

Diphen hydramine hydrochloride	12.5 mg
Colour ama ranth	Q.S
Flavoured syrup base	Q.S
Batch size	100.0 litres
Practical yield	970 bottles
Usual packing	100 ml amber bottles

Formulation:

Sr. No	Ingredient	Quantity
1	Diphenhydramine hydrochloride	255 g
2	Sugar	33 g
3	Sodium benzoate	100 g
4	Citric acid	500 g
5	Saccharin sodium	100 g
6	Colour amaranth	50 g
7	Essence raspberry	200 ml
8	Spirit chloroform	5.0 lit
9	Propylene glycol	2 lit

Manufacturing specifications:

1. pH 4.2 to 4.7
2. Fill in 100 ml amber bottles with 25 mm PP caps

Manufacturing Process

1. Prepare sugar syrup as usual.
2. Dissolve sodium benzoate in water and add to 1.
3. Dissolve saccharin sodium in water and add to 2.
4. Dissolve citric acid in water and add to 3 with stirring.
5. Dissolve amaranth colour in water and add to 4. Check pH, it should be acidic.
6. Dissolve diphen hydramine hydrochloride in water and add to 5 with stirring.
7. Add the essence to 6.
8. Add spirit chloroform to 7 with stirring.

9. Make–up the volume with water, adjust the pH if necessary and fill in amber coloured bottles.

Validation of Liquid Syrup Section

1. *Tanks:* Marked indication of tanks 100 *l*, 200 *l*, 500 *l*, 1000 *l* etc should be periodically validated for accuracy by putting actually measured amount of water.
2. *Stirrer:* Speed and direction of rotation should be watched periodically.
3. *Colloid mill:* Particle size after passing depends on clearance between rotor and stator. It is indicated on scale kept outside. It should be validated periodically. Its direction of rotation to be checked before use.
4. *Measuring:* Used for volume checks of filled bottles should be calibrated correctly at particular temperature and should be periodically validated.
5. Microbial counts of water if increased beyond caution level, it is normally treated with formalin to reduce the microbial load. The standard process should be periodically validated.
6. Filters used for filtration of water in demineralised water plant should also be validated.
7. UV light used at outlet junction of demineralised water plant–record for its burning water to be maintained and its effectiveness should be validated after specific duration

SOLID DOSAGE FORMS

Tablet

Tablets are compressed. Solid dosage forms usually prepared with the aid of suitable pharmaceutical excipients.

Additives used in tablets are as follows:

1 Diluent

2 Glidant, antiadherent

3 Sweetening agent
4 Binders
5 Colorants
6 Flavours (perfumes)
7 Lubricants

These additives are discussed in chapter second.

Preparation Methods for Tablets

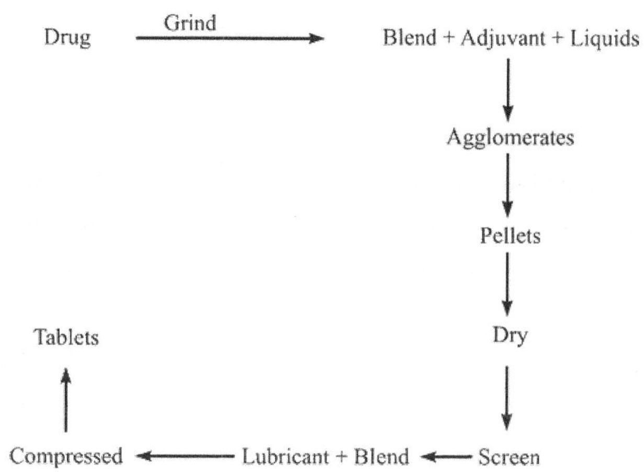

I. Wet granulation

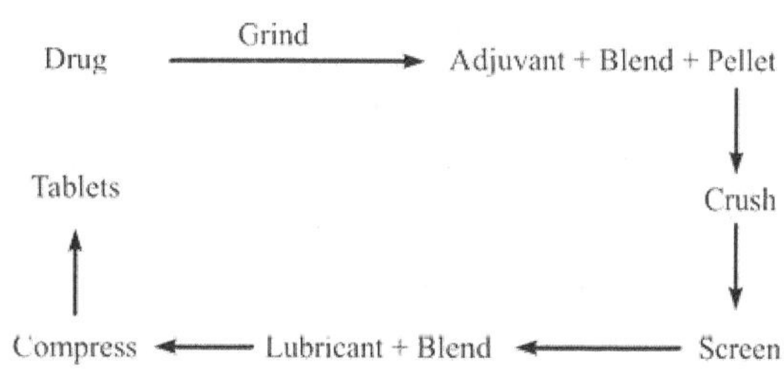

II. Dry granulation

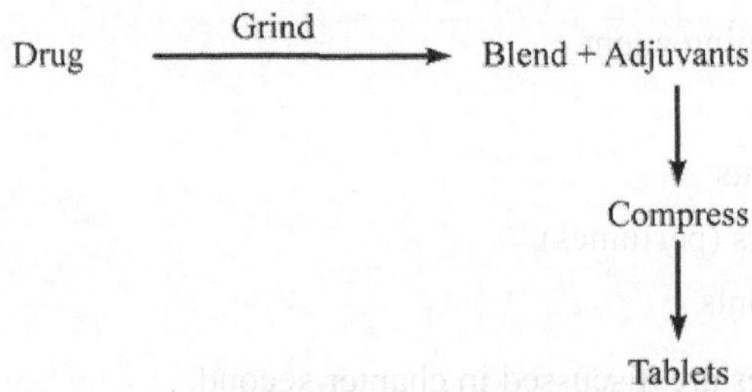

III. Direct compression

Antacid Tablets

Labelled formula:

Each tablet contains:

Dried aluminium hydroxide gel	250	mg
Magnesium hydroxide	250	mg
Activate dimethicone	50	mg
Batch size	50,000	tablets
Practical yield	48500	tablets
Usual packing	strips of 10	tablets

Formulation:

Sr. No	Ingredient	Quantity
1	Dried aluminium hydroxide gel	13.10 kg
2	Magnesium hydroxide	13.10 kg
3	Methyl polysiloxane	2.65 kg
4	Sugar powder	17.00 kg
5	Methyl paraben sodium	100 kg
6	Propyl paraben sodium	50 kg
7	Sugar for syrup	10.00 kg
8	Magnesium stearate	2.00 kg
9	Talcum	2.00 kg
10	Menthol	50 gm
11	Essence orange	8.40 ml

Manufacturing specifications

1. Weight of granules – 60 kg
2. Weight of 20 tablets – 240 gm
3. Weight per tablet – 12 gm
4. Description – white round flat tablets
5. Punch-size – 15 mm
6. Weight variation about 3.5%
7. Friability not more than 1%
8. Hardness not less than 5 kg/cm^2
9. Disintegration does not apply
10. Use pharma grade sugar as diluent

Manufacturing process

1. Transfer aluminium hydroxide gel and magnesium hydroxide to the mixer
2. Add pharma grade sugar
3. Mix for 15 minutes
4. Add activated dimethicone and mix for another 45 minutes
5. Prepare simple syrup with 10 kg sugar and 8 litres water containing methyl paraben sodium and propyl paraben sodium. Allow the sugar syrup to cool to room temperature
6. Add sugar in the mixer and mix for 30 minutes
7. Pass the mass through multimill
8. Dry the granules at 45°C
9. Sieve the granules through no. 16 mesh
10. Mix 4 kg granules with menthol dissolved in about 50 ml chloroform. Also add 8.40 ml of oil orange
11. Lubricate the granules as usual before compression

Antiasthmatic tablets

Labelled formula

Each tablet contains

Phenobarbitone	20 mg
Papavarine	0.01 mg
Aminophylline	100 mg
Batch size	200,000 tablets
Practical yield	194,000 tablets
Usual packing	strip of 10 tablets

Formulation:

Sr. No	Ingredient	Quantity
1	Phenobarbitone	4.00 kg
2	Papaverine	2.0 g
3	Aminophylline	20.00 kg
4	Dicalcium phosphate	9.00 kg
5	Cocoa powder	3.20 kg
6	Starch	10.64 kg
7	Talcum	6.60 kg
8	Magnesium stearate	600 gm
9	Denature sprit	Q.S

Manufacturing process

(i) Mix 9 kg dicalcium phosphate, 4 kg phenobarbitone, 1.3 kg cocoa, 6.14 kg starch and 2 g papaverine in a mixer for 20 minutes.

(ii) Mix 20 kg aminophylline, 9 kg coca, 4.5 kg starch and 6.6 kg talcum in a mixer for 20 minutes

(iii) Dry the granules as usual. Carry out the slugging process. Break the slugs of part I and part II pass through No. 14 sieves. Lubricate the granules as usual and send the granules for compression.

Manufacturing specifications

1. Total weight of granules 54 kg
2. Weight of 20 tablets 5.4 g
3. Weight per tablet 270 mg
4. Disintegration time 15 minutes
5. Punch size 8.5 mm
6. Weight variation less than 3.5%
7. Friability of tablets less than 1%

Anticold Tablets

Labelled formula:

Each tablet contains:

Aspirin	300	mg
Chlorpheniramine maleate	2	mg
Phenylephrine hydrochloride	2.5	mg
Batch size	100,000	tablets
Practical yield	98,000	tablets
Usual packing	strip of 10	tablets

Formulation

Sr. No	Ingredients	Quantity
1	Aspirin	30.0kg
2	Chlorpheniramine maleate	208g
3	Phenylephrine hydro chloride	255g
4	Dicalcium phosphate	15.0kg
5	Starch	16.0kg
6	Methyl carboxy cellulose	2.0kg
7	Magnesium stearate	700g
8	Talcum	2.8kg
9	Gelatin	300g

Manufacturing specifications

1. Total weight – 67 kg
2. Weight per tablet – 670 mg
3. Thickness – 3.8 + 0.2
4. Punch size – 12.6 mm
5. Disintegration timeless than 5 minutes

Manufacturing process

1. Mix aspirin, ½ methyl carboxy cellulose, 300 g. talc and 300 gm magnesium stearate. Feed the material to a slugging machine. Break the slugs to get granules of 16 mesh size.
2. Mix chlorpheniramine maleate, phenylephrine hydrochloride, dicalcium phosphate, starch and undertake wet granulation with a paste of gelatine, 1.2 kg starch and 7.5 litres purified water
3. Mix granules 1 and 2 and lubricate with magnesium stearate, talcum and add balance of methyl carboxy cellulose and dry starch as disintegrating agents.
4. Compress tablets as usual.

FORMULATION FACTORS AFFECTING THE RELEASE OF A DRUG

(i) *The effective surface area of the drug:* To increase the dissolution rate for a given amount of drug, the effective surface area has to be increased. If the drug is hydrophobic a reduction in particle size may produce a smaller effective surface area and a reduction in dissolution rate.

(ii) *Effect of binding agents:* Binding agents coat the drug particles and therefore the rate of solution of the binder in water can determine the release rate from the tableted drug. Tablets containing soluble binders (hydrolysed gelatin and PVP) had rapid dissolution rate whereas slow and incomplete disintegration of tablets formulated with starch paste led to protracted release of drug.

(iii) *Effect of disintegrants:* Disintegrants act by either bursting open the tablet or by promoting the rapid ingress of water into the center of the tablet or capsule. Chlorpropamide tablets containing sodium starch glycollate were superior in dissolution properties from similar tablets containing micro-crystalline cellulose and cross–linked polyvinyl pyrrolidene. The ion exchange resin amberlite was found to promote rapid disintegration of chlorpropamide tablets but dissolution rates were found to be inferior to starch glucollate

(iv) *Effect of lubricants:* The hydrophilic lubricant SLS (sodium lauryl sulphate) allowed the drug to dissolve more rapidly than the control tablet containing no lubricant. Hydrophobic lubricant magnesium stearate produced a decrease in dissolution rate.

(v) *Effect of diluents:* Calcium salts found to be superior to the other diluents. Sorbitol dissolve very slowly and therefore release of the drug occurs by erosion. The calcium salt were shown to promote the rapid disintegration of the tablets and therefore to liberate the drug quickly from the dosage form.

(vi) *Effect of granule size:* This factor affect in vitro and in vivo properties of bendrofluazide tablets 5 mg. In general granule size was not a critical factor affecting the pharmaceutical properties of the tablets.

DIFFICULTIES WHICH MAY OCCUR IN TABLETING

The most common problem encountered during tabletting is capping and chiping. Factors which cause a tablet to cap or chip.

(i) Excess fines or powder which traps air in the table mixture.

(ii) Worn dies

(iii) Too much pressure

(iv) Unsuitable formula

(v) Moist and soft granulation

(vi) Improper aligment of punches

(vii) Worn or imperfect punches

(viii) Deep marking on tablet punches

1. Binding or Sticking in the Dies

Instead of moving freely in the dies tablets may be ejected with difficulty accompanied by noise. Reasons may be:

(i) Granules may be insufficiently or unevenly lubricated. Remixing of granules or extra addition of lubricants may correct this

(ii) Die may be dirty or unpolished

(iii) Granules may have been dried inadequately or have absorbed water vapour. Determination of moisture content of the granules will show whether further drying is necessary

(iv) Die is worn out. Change the old die by new one

2. Picking

This is found when granules adhere to the punch face after compression. It may be due following reasons:

(i) Inadequate or uneven lubrication

(ii) Granules may be under dried

(iii) Punch face may be pitted, scratched or unpolished

3. Capping

This is the problem most frequently occurred in tablet compression and one of the most difficult to correct. It occurs when the top of the tablet or cap becomes detached from the main body either at the time of compression or after the tablet has left the die. Various reasons:

(i) *Use of ringed dies:* Replace the dies caused by constant friction.

(ii) *Speed of compression:* If speed is too rapid, entrapped air is not given time to escape and get trapped within the tablet until released by removal of the pressure. The air then expands and escapes at the periphery, the weakest part of the tablet, detaching the cap as it does so.

(iii) *Presence of excessive fines:* Normally 30 to 35% of fines are tolerated. If fines are more than this then capping may result. This can confirmed by sieve analysis.

(iv) *Punches fitting too closely in the dies:* This may occur with new sets of tools, when air in the granules cannot escape between the upper punch and die wall. This can be corrected by very slightly reducing the diameter of the upper punches by grinding.

(v) *Use of excessive pressure*: The pressure applied should only be sufficient to give tablets of adequate hardness. Excessive pressure may not only adversely affect D.T. but if applied beyond the limit of elasticity of the granules, will cause slight expansion of tablets after pressure is released and capping might occur.

(vi) *Influence of binder:* This may be less in quantity than required or may not be suitable for particular drug. In either cases the granules will be friable and lacking in cohesion.

(vii) *Over drying of granules:* This is a frequent cause as granules require certain moisture content, varying with different drugs to assist the action of the binder in producing a hard tablet.

(viii) *Physical form of drugs:* Sulfanilamide in anhydrous form persistently capped when compressed while partly hydrated form could be compressed without difficulty using the some excipients in both cases.

It is known that certain crystalline forms cause capping although granules may be satisfactory in every respect. In such cases, crystal structure must be destroyed by pulverization before moist granulation e.g., paracetamol tablets.

VALIDATION OF SOLID (TABLET) SECTION

1. *Mixer (planetary or ribbon).* For wet mass preparation. Validate its capacity with a duration of 3 or 6 months.
2. *Shifter:* Put record of sieves used validate for correct size.

3. *Fluidized bed dryer:* Thermometers are checked, FBD trolley cleaned after fixed duration.
4. *Blender:* Lubrication is carriesd out in double cone blender. Checks its rotation per minute.
5. *Compression machines:* Check the speed at which machine run and record of same.
6. *Disintegration Test Apparatus:* Check thermostat and water temperature and check up down movements per minute and keep a record.
7. *Friability apparatus:* Check the rotation per minute and keep a record. Check the timer and record it every week repeated.
8. *Balances:* Zero should be checked before use and weekly record of same is to be maintained.

Chart diagram for validation of process and system

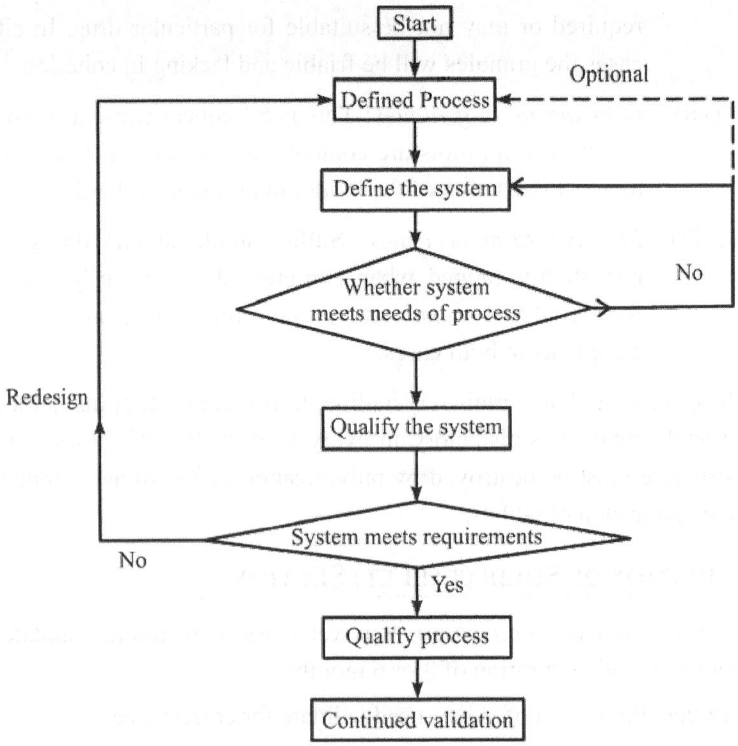

Validation helps to identify root causes of problems and document that the product is made by a reliable manufacturing process. Before conducting process validation following steps must be documented first:

1. *Installation qualification(I.Q):* verification of key aspects of the installation recommended for design.
2. *Operational qualification(O.Q):* System performs according to approved operating ranges
3. *Performance qualification(P.Q):* Product produce from the process will meet its predetermined specifications

Following steps in the process validation:

I *Protocol:* written plan that are followed:

   A. Process description

   B. Process performance qualifications

   C. IQ/OQ cross reference

   D. Environmental qualifications cross–reference

   E. Stability data

II *Protocol approval:* Protocol is seen and discussed by all participating group and final approval given by QC manager.

III *Validation exercise:* Carrry out protocol and collect data, reject non-conforming lots if non-conforming results occur then determine the cause and adjust the process and prepare new protocol.

IV *Validation package preparation:* Study and evaluate data from the validation process, compare it against acceptance criteria and prepare final package for approval.

V Validation approval: Participating group study final package and final approval given by QC manager.

Design Qualifications Format

1. Equipment descriptions
2. References–(i) Specifications, (ii) Quotation, (iii) Order number.

3. Machine specifications
4. Approvals
5. Manual
6. Certifications

Installation Qualification Format

1. Equipment name and make location
2. Approval
3. Description of equipment
4. List of accessories
5. Calibration of equipment used for testing
6. Check list of items
7. List of document
8. Item-wise material of construction
9. List of utilities
10. Summary and report

Operational Qualification Format

1. Equipment name, make and location
2. Approval
3. Description of equipment
4. Calibration status
5. Operation–identity operation under examination
6. Function of key parameters
7. Testing of safety features
8. Summary and report

Performance Qualification Format

1. Equipment name, make and location
2. Approval

3. Objective: Purpose, Responsibility, Reason for qualification and Requalification
4. Related documents
5. Equipment detail
6. Experimental plan
7. Acceptance criteria
8. Tables

Sterile Area Section Validation

Air system, water supply, electrical network must be validated.

In sterile area following things are validated:

(a) *Hepa filter*: Check its efficiency. Particulate count is necessary. Efficiency checked by DOP test

(b) *Autoclave*: Temperature indicator and pressure gauge validated after certain duration.

(c) *Dry heat sterilizer*: Validation of temperature inside it by using thermal probes.

Validation of Filtration Section

(a) Types and porosity of filters

(b) Integrity results before and after

(c) If filter changed then recorded

In case of wet Granulation Process

1. Dry mix time
2. Wet mass preparation time
3. F.B.D drying time
4. Final blending time

These should be standarized and validated after certain duration.

CHAPTER 6

PERFORMANCE EVALUATION METHODS

IN-VITRO DISSOLUTION STUDIES FOR SOLID DOSAGE FORMS

In–vitro dissolution test developed to find out bioavailability of drug product, because *in vivo* method is costly, tedious and time consuming, so this method developed and final result is correlated with the *in vivo* result. *In vitro* dissolution test done outside the body using dissolution test apparatus. During test internal body environment is created outside with dissolution test apparatus.

Factors that must be considered in the design of a dissolution test, are as follows

(a) Factors relating to test apparatus design: size and shape of container, its capacity, agitation type

(b) Factors relating to the dissolution fluid i.e., composition, volume, temperature, sink or non sink

(c) Processing parameters such as sampling technique, dissolution fluid changing etc.

Methods

(i) Rotating basket method–official methods

(ii) Rotating paddle method–official methods

(iii) Beaker method

(iv) Flask stirrer method

(v) Rotating and static disc methods

(i) *Rotating basket Method*

As shown in Fig 6.1 this consist of cylindrical vessel, made up of borosilicate glass or other transparent material, have hemispherical bottom and capacity 1000 ml. Motor is fitted with a stirring basket. The distance between the inside bottom of the vessel and the basket is maintained at 23 to 27 mm during the test. The vessel has a flanged upper rim, fitted with a lid that has number of opening, one is central.

Procedure: In this method place tablet or capsule inside the stainless steel wire basket, which is rotated at a fixed speed while immersed in the dissolution fluid. Samples of the dissolution medium are removed at fixed interval, filtered and assayed.

Note: Dissolution medium free from air and tablet surface also free from air, warm the medium when stated at 36.5 and 37.5

(ii) *Rotating paddle method*

Assembly is same as rotating basket, only there is a difference, agitation is provided by a rotating paddle and dosage form is allowed to sink to the bottom of dissolution vessel before agitation starts.

(iii) *Beaker method*

In this method 400 cm^3 beaker with 250 dm^3 dissolution fluid, agitation is carried out by three bladed polyethylene stirrer with a 50 mm diameter.

The stirrer immersed 27 mm depth into the dissolution medium and rotate at 60 rpm. Tablets drops into the beaker, samples of liquid removed at fixed interval of time, filtered and assayed the solution.

(iv) *Flask stirrer method*

Same as above only round bottom flask used instead of beaker.

(v) *Rotating and static disc methods*

In these methods sample compound compressed into a non-disintegrating disc which is mounted in a holder so that only one face of the disc is exposed. The holder and disc are immersed in the dissolution medium and either held in a fixed position (static disc method) or rotated at a fixed speed. Samples of the dissolution fluid are removed after fixed intervals, filtered and assayed.

For example: Dissolution condition for sustained release tablets

Apparatus – USP XXI; Rotating basket, paddle

Rotational speed – 50 rpm

Dissolution medium – Varies

Temperature – 37 ± 0.5°C

Number of dosage units – Twelve

Sampling schedule – various sampling times, not less than 75 – 80% drug release % dissolved specification – As established

The in vitro dissolution test is important for the purpose of:

(a) Providing necessary process control
(b) Determining stability of the relevant release characteristics of the product
(c) Facilitating certain regulatory determinations and judgements concerning minor formulation changes, changes in site of manufacture etc

In vitro variables compared with *in-vivo* data in *In-vitro – In-vivo* correlations.

Invitro Data

(a) Intrinsic dissolution rate
(b) Drug in solution at a given time
(c) At a time how much drug dissolve in-vitro i.e $t_{58\%}$ to $t_{60\%}$ i.e time for 58 to 60% drug to dissolve.
(d) Plots % dissolution / time
(e) Plots rate of dissolution / time
(f) Rate constants

These data are correlated with *in-vivo* data

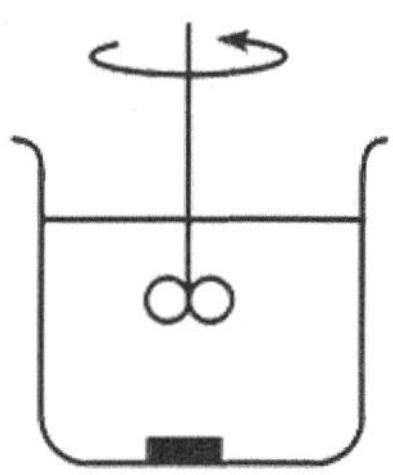

Beaker method

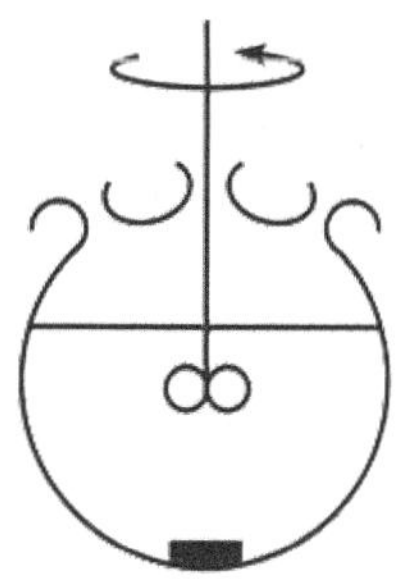

Flask stirrer method

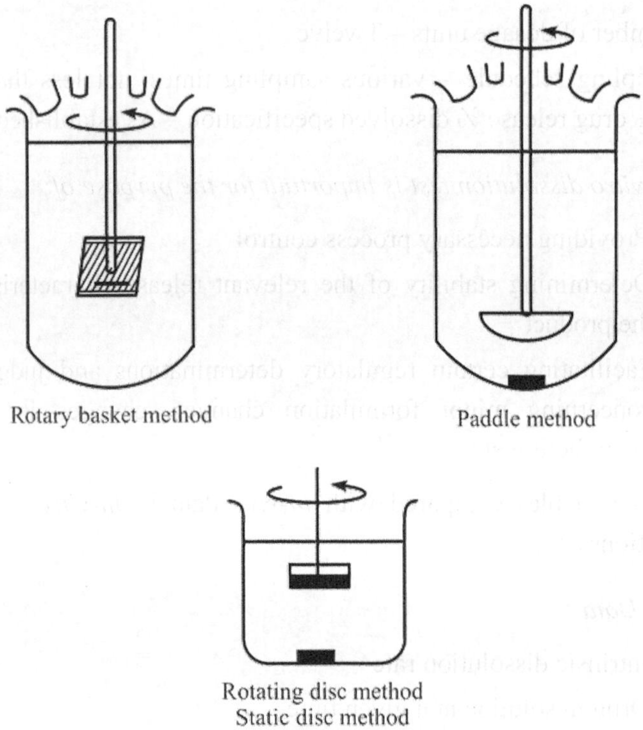

Fig. 6.1 Methods of measuring dissolution rates.

IN VIVO METHODS OF EVALUATION

Bioavailability describes the rate and extent to which an active drug ingredient is absorbed from a drug product and become available at the site of drug action.

Bioequivalence refers to the comparison of bioavailabilities of different formulations, drug products or batches of the same drug product.

Objectives of the bioavailability studies

(a) Important part in new product development

(b) To find out factors which affect absorption of drug

(c) New formulation for an existing drug

(d) Q/C measure, absorption is affected by storage condition and stability.

By using bioavailability data we can determined

(a) The amount of drug absorb from a dosage form

(b) The rate at which drug was absorbed

(c) The duration of the drug present in the body fluid

(d) The relationship between drug blood levels and clinical efficacy and toxicity.

GENERAL ELEMENTS OF A BIOAVAILABILITY STUDY

(A) Protocol

(B) Data

(C) Results

(D) Summary and conclusion (discussion)

A. Protocol

(i) Objectives

(ii) Study design

(iii) Subject selection criteria

(iv) Subject exclusion criteria

(v) Type of biological samples

  (a) Sampling times

  (b) Description of sample handling procedures

(vi) Sample inclusion and exclusion criteria

(vii) Ethical consideration

  (a) Subject informed consent form

  (b) Emergency procedures

B. Data

(i) Case reports

(ii) Analytical data for validation of assay method

(iii) Analytical data for biological samples

C. Results

(i) Summary of individual subject data

(ii) Statistical analysis along with summary of statistics

(a) For each individuals sample times

(b) For AUC, C_{max}, absorption rate constant (Ka) and elimination rate constant(Ke)

(c) For T_{max} with appropriate method

(iii) Detectable difference at alpha 0.05 and power = 0.80

(iv) 45% symmetrical confidence interval

(v) Application of 75/75 rule to C_{max} and AUC

D. Summary (discussion) and conclusion:

Methods for measurements of Bioavailability

1. Pharmacokinetic methods
   (a) Plasma level time studies
   (b) Urinary excretion studies

2. Pharmacodynamic methods
   (a) Acute Pharmacologic response
   (b) Therapeutic response

1. *Plasma level time studies*

Drug is given orally or i.v and reading of plasma concentration starts. Parameters which are determined in this studies are:

(a) C_{max} → Peak plasma concentration

(b) t_{max} → Peak time

(c) AUC → Area under the curve gives amount of drug in the systemic circulation

Extent of bioavailability can be determined by equations i and ii

$$F_r = \frac{[AUC]_{oral} D_{iv}}{[AUC]_{iv} D_{oral}} \quad .....(i)$$

$$F_r = \frac{[AUC]_{test} D_{std}}{[AUC]_{std} D_{test}} \quad .....(ii)$$

D → Dose administered

i.v → intravenous route

oral → route

std → standard dose

test → test dose

2. *Urinary excretion studies:*

Drug concentration in urinary is studied. In this study, data obtained with a single dose study are:

(i) $\left(\frac{dx_u}{dt}\right)_{max}$: Maximum urinary excretion rate

(ii) (tU_{max}): Time of maximum excretion rate

(iii) X_u: Cumulative amount of drug excreted in urine

The extent of bioavailability can be determined from the equations: iii and iv

$$F = \frac{\left(X_u^{\infty}\right)_{oral} D_{iv}}{\left(X_u^{\infty}\right)_{iv} D_{oral}} \quad .....(iii)$$

$$Fr = \frac{\left(X_u^{\infty}\right)_{test} D_{std}}{\left(X_u^{\infty}\right)_{std} D_{test}} \quad .....(iv)$$

3. Acute pharmacologic response can be measured by measuring any pharmacological response produced by the drug in the body. Disadvantage is that, pharmacological varies.

4. Therapeutic response is measured by observing the clinical response produced by the drug. Disadvantage is that quantitation of observed response is not possible.

In vitro – In vivo correlation

1. Correlations based on plasma level data
2. Correlation based on the urinary excretion data
3. Correlation based on the pharmacologic response

Statistical moments theory can also be used to determine relationship such as mean dissolution time (*in vitro*) versus mean residence time (*in vivo*)

Invitro – invivo correlation help in batch to batch consistency and a tool in development of a new dosage form.

Factors influencing bioavailability of orally administered drugs:

1. Drug substance physiochemical properties
   - (i) Particle size
   - (ii) crystalline or amorphous form
   - (iii) Hydration
   - (iv) pH and pKa
   - (v) Lipid and water solubility
2. Pharmaceutical ingredients and dosage form characteristics
   - (i) Ingredients such as fillers, binders, coatings, lubricants, disintegrants, suspending agents, surface active agents, flavouring agents, colouring agents, preservative agents, stabilizing agents
   - (ii) Disintegration rate of dosage form

(iii) Dissolution time of drug in dosage form
(iv) Product age and storage conditions

3. Physiological factors and patient characteristic
   (i) Gastric emptying time
   (ii) Intestinal transit time
   (iii) Gastro intestinal abnormality
   (iv) Gastric contents such as food and fluids
   (v) Gastro intestinal pH
   (vi) Drug metabolism (Through gut and during first passage through liver)

BIOEQUIVALENCE STUDY OF DRUG PRODUCTS

Bioequivalence is defined as, "the drug substance in two or more identical dosage forms, which reaches the systemic circulation at the same relative rate and to the same plasma concentration time curves without any statistical differences."

The following terms are used by FDA to define level of equivalency between drug products:

1. *Pharmaceutical equivalents:* These are the drug products which contain identical amounts of identical active drug ingredient, i.e., the same salt or ester of the same therapeutic moiety in identical dosage forms.
2. *Chemical equivalents:* These drug products contain same labelled chemical substance as an active ingredient in the same amount.
3. Pharmaceutical alternatives: These drug products contain the identical therapeutic group, or its precursor, but not in the same amount or dosage form or as the same salt or ester.
4. *Bioequivalent drug products:* These are the pharmaceutical equivalents or pharmaceutical alternatives whose rate and

extent of absorption do not show a significance difference when administered at the same molar dose of therapeutic moiety under similar experimental conditions (either single dose or multiple dose)

5. *Therapeutic equivalents:* These drug products indicate pharmaceutical equivalents, which, when administered to the same individuals in the same dosage regimens, will provide the same therapeutic effect.

The rate and extent to which a drug in a dosage form becomes available for biological absorption generally depends upon the materials utilized in the formulation and also on the method of manufacture. Thus, the same drug when formulated in different dosage forms possesses different bioavailability characteristics and exhibits different clinical effectiveness.

STATISTICAL INTERPRETATION OF BIOEQUIVALENCE DATA

The statistical data of bioequivalence study is collected and determined by a method known as cross–over design study method (A Latin square method).

This method involves the study and administration of a single dose of test and reference formulations by the same route in equal doses at different times to determine the relative bioavailability. The study is performed in fasting, young, healthy and adult male volunteers. Then, the patient population data is collected and tabulated and the parameters used to assess and compare bioavailability [i.e. C_{max}, t_{max}, AUC (area under the curve)] are then analyzed with statistical procedures.

An analysis of variance (ANOVA) test method is generally applied to determine the level in the rate and extent of absorption between two or more drug products. If the relative bioavailability of test formulation is within the range 80–120% of reference standard product, it is considered bioequivalent.

Note: Under 1984 act, to gain FDA approval a generic drug product must:

(i) Be bioequivalent

(ii) Meet the same batch-to-batch requirements for identity, strength, purity and quality

(iii) Have the same indications and precautions for use and other labelling instructions

(iv) Contain the same active ingredients as the pre-formulized drug

(v) Be identical in strength, dosage form enroute of administration.

CHAPTER 7

STANDARD OPERATING PROCEDURES, PROCESS OPTIMIZATION, NEW PRODUCT LAUNCH

STANDARD OPERATING PROCEDURES (SOPs)

These are written procedures that describe how to perform basic operations in plant. The procedures should be written in simple language that untrained new personnel should be able to understand and follow these procedures.

SOP's is applicable for machine, equipments, cleaning, test or for any procedures.

The SOP should contain:

1. *Objective:* This explain the application SOP
2. *Responsibility:* The person who is responsible to follow that SOP

3. *Accountability:* The person who is responsible for the procedure or for responsible person
4. *Procedure:* Actual procedure (operating procedure) which must be followed.

SOPS FOR SOME IDEAL FORMULATIONS

Solid dosage form e.g., tablet

Co-trimoxazale double strength tablet

Trimethoprim (TMP)	16.00 kg
Sulfamethoxazole	80.00 kg
Maize starch	14.00 kg
Polyvinyl pyrrdidene (PVP)	0.5 kg
Sodium lauryl sulphate	0.4 kg
Maize. Starch	1.00 kg
Magnesium stearate	0.900 kg
	112.800 kg

Batch size: 100,000

TABLETS

SOP:

1. Sieve TMP and sulfamethoxazole through 60 no. sieve, maize starch through 100 no. and Magnesium Stearate through 60 no. sieve.
2. *Dry mixing:* Dry mix TMP and sufomethoxazole and Maize starch (14.00 kg) for 30 min in a mixer
3. *Paste preparation:* Boil 12lit of deionized water, add PVP, discontinue the heating when PVP is completely dissolved. Cool to 45°C. Add sodium lauryl sulphate (SLS) suspended in 500 ml of water
4. *Wet mixing:* Time–10 min, (add extra DI water if required)

5. *Wet milling:* Pass the wet mass through 8 no. on cadmach granulator
6. *Drying:* Dry the milled mass in a tray dryer at 60°C for 5 to 6 hours
7. *Dry screening:* Pass the dried granules through sieve no. 16 on mechanical sifter pass the granule through sieve no. 12 on cadmach granulator
8. *Lubrication:* Load the batch into drum blender, mix for 5 min. Collect the fines of 60 no. and mix with mg. stearate. (60 no.) and Maize starch (100 no.), load in drum blender and blend for 5 min.
9. Batch is ready for compression

Liquid dosage form e.g syrup

Liquid protein B-complex

Batch size – 500 lit

pH – 5.1

1.	Protein hydrolysate	317.42	kg
2.	Sugar	250.0	kg
3.	$FeSO_4H_2O$	2.5	kg
4.	Follic acid	0.033	kg
5.	Vitamin B_{12}	0.666	gm
6.	Vitamin B_1	0.166	kg
7.	Vitamin B_2 sodium	0.148	kg
8.	Vitamin B_6	0.367	kg
9.	Niacinamide	0.958	kg
10.	D. panthenol	0.150	kg
11.	Nipagin sodium	0.60	kg
12.	Nipasol sodium	0.300	kg

13.	Saccharin sodium	0.500	kg
14.	Citric acid	0.050	kg
15.	Disodium EDTA	5.600	kg
16.	Colour carmel	5.00	kg
17.	Essence butter scotch	0.50	kg
18.	Essence cardamom	0.50	kg
19.	Essence raspberry	0.50	lit
20.	Water to make (q.s.)	500.00	lit

Procedure: (SOP)

1. Heat demineralize water + sugar + nipagin sodium + nipasol sodium + saccharin sodium (i)
2. Add protein hydrolysate to (i)
3. Add $FeSO_4$ after dissolving to (i)
4. Dissolve in water Vitamin B_{12} + Vitamin B_1 + Vitamin B_2 sod + Vitamin B_6 + niacinamine + dpanthenol separately add to (i)
5. Dissolve folic acid in water and add to (i)
6. Dissolve citric acid and EDTA in water and add to (i)
7. Add colour carmel and other essence to final solution and adjust the volume, stir for 30 min.

Semisolid dosage form e.g ointment:

Skin care ointment: Batch size 300 gm

1.	Oil extract	150	gm
2.	Bees wax	48	gm
3.	Water	99.6	gm
4.	Borax	2.4	gm
5.	Nipagin sodium	30	mg
6.	Nipasol sodium	10	mg
7.	B.H.A	250	mg
8.	Perfume jasmine	4	ml

Procedure: (SOP's)

1. Heat oil extract + Bees wax + B.H.A (antioxidant) to 80°C
2. Heat water + borax + nipagin + nipasol upto 80°C. At 70°C add (1) to (2) while constantly stirring
3. When temperature at 40°C add jasmine 4 ml and stir. Cool the mixture to room temperature and fill it in collapsible tube.

CHLORAMPHENICAL SUSPENSION

Batch size – 400lit and pH 5.6

1.	Chloramphenicol palmitate	17.360	kg
2.	Sodium citrate	4.00	kg
3.	Citric acid	0.4	gm
4.	Sodium saccharin	0.48	kg
5.	Nipagin sodium	0.520	kg
6.	Nipasol sodium	0.200	kg
7.	Sodium C.M.C	3.00	kg
8.	Sugar	160.0	kg
9.	Essence banana	1.0	lit

Procedure: (SOPs)

1. Deionized water + sugar + nipagin sodium + nipasol sodium sodium + sodium saccharin + citric acid + sodium citrate – solution A
2. Deionized water + sodium CMC + Chloramphenical plamifate homogenise – solution B
3. Add solution A and solution B while homogenizing solution is obtained
4. Add essence

RIFAMPICIN CAPSULE 150 mg

Batch size – 200,000; size of capsule 2

1. Rifampicin — 30.6 kg with overages
2. Maize starch (dried) — 20.0 kg
3. Magnesium stearate — 1.00 kg

Total = 51.60 kg

Average weight per capsule 258 mg

Mix all the material after passing through sieve of 40 no. for 30 min. and fill the powder in capsule and check the average weight. Hand machine or semiautomatic machine will be utilized.

OTHER EXAMPLES OF SOPs

Atropine eye ointment

Labelled formula:

Atropine sulphate

In a sterile eye ointment base – 0.1% w/w

Batch size – 20 kg

Practical yield – 5500 tubes

Usual packing – 3.5 gm aluminium collapsible tubes

Formulation

sssss	Ingredient	Quantity
1	Atropine sulphate	200 g
2	Liquid paraffin	1 kg
3	Cetostearyl alcohol	1 kg
4	Hard paraffin	1 kg
5	White soft paraffin	16.8 kg

Manufacturing specifications:

1. Aluminium collapsible tubes should be dipped in a mixture of isopropyl alcohol 70% containing 0.022% of benzylkonium chloride for 10 to 15 minutes for sterilization. Keep these tubes in previously sterilised trays.
2. Expose the washed and treated tubes to fumes of formalin. Fumigation can be done with $KMnO_4$ and formalin in a chamber for 24 hours.
3. Filling of tubes to be done aseptically.

Manufacturing process:

1. Melt cetostearyl alcohol, hard paraffin and white soft paraffin along with liquid paraffin. Heat at 150°C for atleast 1 hour for effective sterilization of ointment base. Allow the mass to cool to a semi-solid state under aseptic conditions. Mixed base should be filtered before cooling.
2. Dissolve atropine sulphate in 200ml of sterilized water for injections and add to the semi solid sterilized base under continuous mixing and aseptic conditions.
3. Fill in sterile tubes.

Dexamethasone eye/ ear drops:

Labelled formula:

1. Dexamethasone	0.1% w/v (as dexamethasone sodium phosphate)
2. Phenylethyl alcohol	0.25% w/v
3. Phenyl mercuric nitrate	0.02% w/v
Batch size	10 litres
Practical yield	8750 vials
Usual packing	3 ml Amber vials

Formulations:

Sr. No.	Ingredients	Quantity
1.	Dexamethasone Sodium Phosphate	12.4 g
2.	Creatinin	120 g
3.	Sodium metabisulphate	48 g
4.	Sodium borate	30 g
5.	Sodium citrate	100 g
6.	Phenyl mercuric nitrate	200 mg
7.	Phenylethyl alcohol	25 ml
8.	Water for injection to	10 lit.

Manufacturing specifications

1. pH range 7.2 to 7.8
2. Use butyl, latex or neoprene rubber stoppers
3. Shelf life 18 months
4. Use 3ml amber vials
5. Sterilize vials at 200°C for 4 hours
6. Sterilize rubber stoppers in autoclave at 121°C for 30 minutes
7. Filter the solution through G–4 sintered glass funnel and finally through 0.2 membrane filter
8. All manufacturing, filling and sealing to be done under strict aseptic conditions.

Manufacturing process:

1. Dissolve phenyl mercuric nitrate 200mg in 1 litre distilled water.
2. Dissolve sodium citrate in 1 litre distilled water.
3. Dissolve sodium metabisulphite and sodium borate in sufficient distilled water.
4. Mix 1, 2 and 3 to phenyletheyl alcohol to solution.

5. Make up the volume to 9.9 litre.
6. Filter the in process solution through filtration pad followed G–4 sintered glass funnel.
7. Autoclave the in process solution at 121°C for 20 minutes.
8. Dissolve the dexamethasone sodium phosphate and creatinin in this sterile solution.
9. Adjust the pH between 7.5 to 8.5 with sterile NaOH solution if required.
10. Adjust the volume to 10 litre with sterile distilled water.
11. Filter first through G–4 sintered glass funnel and then through 0.2 membrane filter.
12. Fill in 3 ml vials with pre and post nitrogen flushing
13. Fill under strict aseptic conditions.

ANTISEPTIC CREAM

Labelled formula

Gamma benzene hexa chloride – 0.1% w/w

Proflavine – 0.1% w/w

Batch – 100 kg

Practical yield – 3800 tubes

Usual packing – 25 g tubes

Formulations:

Sr. No	Ingredient	Quantity
1	Gama benzene hexachloride	102 g
2	Proflavine	102 g
3	Cetosteryl alcohol	10 kg
4	Cetomgragol 1000	2.5 kg
5	Liquid paraffin	8.0 kg
6	Purified water	80 kg

Manufacturing process:

1. Heat cetostearyl alcohol, cetomegragol 1000 and 6 kg of liquid paraffin to 110°C.
2. Heat purified water to 60°C–70°C and add to 1st step with the aid of emulsifier.
3. Suspend gama benzene hexachloride in 2 kg of liquid paraffin and add to step 2 with constant stirring.
4. Dissolve proflavine in sufficient purified water and to the mass under stirring.
5. Mix the yellow soft mass for 2–3 hours.

Note: Proflavine changes to orange colour on exposure to light.

CHLORAMPHNICOL EAR DROPS

Labelled formula:

Chloromphenicol – 5%

Benzocaine – 1%

Batch size – 10 litres

Practical yield – 970 vials

Usual packing – 10 ml amber vials

Formulation

Sr. No	Ingredient	Quantity
1	Chloromphenicol	510 g
2	Benzocaine	100 g
3	Propylene glycol to (q.s.)	10 litre

Manufacturing process

1. Dissolve benzocaine in 5 litre, propylene glycol at 60°C.
2. Add chloramphenicol to step (1) in small portions with stirring to dissolve completely.
3. Make up the volume to 10 litres with propylene glycol.

PROCEE OPTIMIZATION

Optimization means to make as perfect; effective or functional as possible, in this, there is implementation of systematic approaches to achieve the best combination process characteristics under a given set of condition

Advantages of optimization techniques:

1. Best solution can be obtained
2. Easily problems can be found out and corrected
3. In this technique, time, material and cost are saved
4. In this technique, by conducting few experiments best results are obtained
5. By this technique process development can be achieved and subsequent scale up

VARIABLES

During drug product design and development various parameters involved are known as variables. These are two types of variables:

1. Independent variable i.e., input variables under development scientist control e.g., mixing time, excipient amount etc.
2. Dependent variables i.e., characteristics of final product or in process product known as dependent variables e.g., friability, size of granules, dissolution time etc.

Factors defined as independent variables which affect the formulation characteristics or output of the process.

Effect defined as the factor level varied, net response obtained is changed.

Interaction occurs when more than two or two factors depend on each other.

Orthogonality is the effect due to main factors and independent of interactions, lack of orthogonality termed confounding.

Factor space which is defined as dimensional space by the coded variables.

OPTIMIZATION PROCESS (TYPE)

1. *Simultaneous optimization methodology*: In this, experiments continue before the optimization takes place
2. *Sequential optimization methodology*: In this, experiments continue sequentially as the optimization study proceeds.

Simultaneous optimization methodology: Also known as response surface methodology, this is a model dependent technique. In this technique main factor, experimental design, models and graphic results. In this one or more experimental results obtained, noted to predict the optimum and interaction effects. Then mathematical model for each response is determined and obtained.

Experimental Design

1. Factorial design and modification
2. Centre composite design and modification
3. Mixture design
4. D. Optimal design

    1. Factorial design (FD) and modification based on first degree mathematical model. In full FDs there is studying of all the factors, including their interaction among them. In simplest FD only two factors are studied at two levels.
    2. Central composite design (CCD) and its modifications: In this design for 2nd order models are involved CCD involved the combination of a two-level factorial point and a central point.

3. Mixture design (MD) In this factors considered can not varied simultaneously and result noted at each level, like in FDs and CCD, simplex design is preferred
4. D. Optimal design are used when the domain is irregular in shape

   Hence in RSM there is model selection and search for an optimum is carry out.

SEQUENTIAL OPTIMIZATION METHODOLOGY

In this method no need of planning all the experiments simultaneously, prior knowledge of response surface is not essential.

Methods:

1. Steepest ascent method
2. Optimum path method
3. Sequential simplex techniques
4. Evolutionary operations.

   1. *Steepest ascent (decent) methods* are methods for I^{st} order design.
   2. *In optimum path method* like steepest ascent method, where optimum is also found outside the experimental domain by extrapolation.
   3. *Sequential simplex method* is model independent method. In this data obtained from experiments and based upon response and rule one result obtained, upon which new experiment performed.
   4. *Evolutionary operations* This process is progress in such a way that produces the product and at the same time provides information on product improvement. For this there is factorial and simplex design and a large number of experiments are carriedout.

Table 7.1 optimization method under various situations.

Methods	Model for use and degree
1. Graphical analysis	Model for any order. More than 4 factors and gives single response
2. Steepest ascent	1st order model, single response and optimum outside the domain
3. Optimum path	2nd order model, optimum outside the domain and single response
4. Sequential simplex	No model, direct optimization and single or multiple response
5. Evolutionary simplex	Industrial situation; slight variation possible

NEW PRODUCT LAUNCH

New drug means any drug (except a new animal drug or an animal feed bearing or containing a new animal drug) the composition of which is such among experts qualified, by scientific training and experience to evaluate the safety and effectiveness of drugs, as safe and effective for use under the conditions prescribed, recommended or suggested in the labelling there of, except that such a drug not so recognised shall not be deemed to be a "new drug"; if at any time prior to the enactment of this act it was subject to the Food and Drugs Acts of June, 30th 1906, as amended and if at such time its labelling contained the same representation concerning the conditions of its use.

Any drug (except a new animal drug or in animal feed bearing or containing a new animal drug) the composition of which is such that such drug, as a result of investigations to determine its safety and effectiveness for use under such conditions, has become so recognised but which has not, otherwise that in such investigations been used as a material extent or for a material time under such condition.

INTRODUCTION OF NEW DRUG

Basic requirement is safety and effectiveness. Adequate and well controlled investigation including clinical investigations by experts qualified by scientific training and experience to evaluate the effectiveness of the drug involved to suggest its potency in particular disease.

A drug may be considered "new" because of its composition, its use, its dosage, or its dosage form. Active ingredient with new chemical entity can be considered as "new drug". Drug may also be new owing to its composition of inactive ingredients, the proportion of ingredients, and combination of ingredients active or inactive. A drug recommended new use or change in recommended dosage, dosage form, or route of administration also can cause it to be considered a "new drug". The basis for a drug's 'newness' determines what steps must be taken to obtain an approved new drug application.

When any new chemical moiety is identified, 'the preclinical testing' is done in animals. When the drug is found effective and safe in animals test the permission to do clinical trials in human being is undertaken and tests carried out. All reports are collected and when experts declared that drug is safe and effective, permission to use in mass public is given.

The new drug application to FDA includes:

1. Detailed report of preclinical studies
2. Reports of clinical studies
3. Information on the drug and on the controls and facilities used in its manufacture
4. Samples of drugs and its labelling

If any change is made, in packaging, manufacturing, labelling, colour, additional information, expiry date should be reported to FDA immediately. In new drug application, information regarding actual formula with quantity, place of manufacturing, supplier of ingredients, persons involved in process, facility control, Good Manufacturing Practices standards, test for identity, purity, analytical methods must be specified. For new drug 5 years patent protection is given.

Chart shows new drug development process.

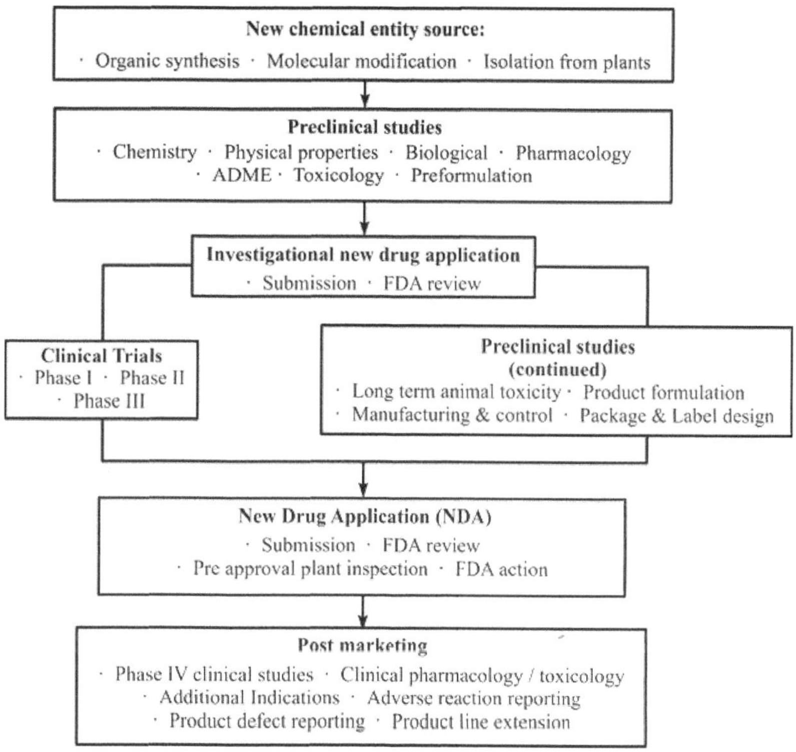

Further Readings

1. Remington's Pharmaceutical Sciences; Mack publishing company.
2. Matrix A.N., Swarbrick J. and Commarata, A., Physical Pharmacy; Lea and Febiger.
3. Bean, H.S; Beckett, A.H. and Carless, J.E., Avancees in Pharmaceutical Sciences, Vol.2 ; Academic press.
4. Lachman, L; Liebermann, H.A.; Kanig, J.L; theory and Practice of Industrial Pharmacy; Lea and Febiger.
5. Martin, E.W; Dispensing of Medications; Mack Publishing Company.
6. Ansel, H.C., Introduction to pharmaceutical Dosage Forms; Lea and Febiger.
7. Handbook of Pharmaceutical Excipients, Pharmaceutical Press; London.
8. The Drugs and Cosmetics Act and Rules; Govt. of India Publication.

9. Liebermann, H.A., and Lachmann, L; Tablets; Vols. I, II and II, Mercel Dekker, NewYork.
10. Gunn, C. and Carter, S.J; Dispensing for Pharmaceutical Students; Kothari Book Depot, Mumbai.
11. British Pharmacopoeia (Edition-2007), HMSO, London.
12. Indian Pharmacopoeia, 2007, Edition-5th, New Delhi.
13. United States Pharmacopoeia – National Formulary.